Rogers J. Greene Jr.

Warning: This material is spiritually discerned.

Our light is an expression of His glory.

Rogers J. Greene Jr.

Jasher Press & Co.

Published By:
Jasher Press & Co.
www.jasherpress.com
P.O. Box 14520
New Bern, NC 28561

Copyright© 2011
Interior Text Design by Pamela S. Almore
Cover Design by Pamela S. Almore

ISBN: 978-0615510033
Pages of Light Vol. 1
All rights reserved. Except for brief excerpts used in reviews, no portion of this work may be reproduced or published without expressed written permission from the author of the author's agent.

First Edition
Printed and bound in the United States of America

Copyright © 2011 Rogers J. Greene Jr.
All rights reserved. Except as permitted under the U.S. Copyright Act of 1976, no part of this publication may be reproduced, distributed, or transmitted in any form or by any means, or stored in a database or retrieval system, without the prior written permission of the publisher. The KJV of the bible is used for scripture references unless otherwise indicated in this publication.

Dedication

This writing is dedicated in honor of God our Father and Jesus our savior. As well, I thank God for the influence of my maternal grandfather who loved me with the love of the Lord.

This writing is also dedicated to my spiritual fathers over the past 16 years, Pastor/ Dr. Leon C Jones (Deceased), who was my first Pastor/mentor in the gospel, Bishop W.W. Hackett (Deceased), who added spiritual depth and power to my ministry, and his wife Joyce Hackett, who is still a mentor and source of wisdom for my life and ministry. Thank you to Apostle William Osborne who is a giant in the gospel who has shared more than 40 years of his ministry experiences with me.

I would also like to thank my brothers and sisters in Christ from M.L.K Baptist church in Renton, WA, where I preached my first sermon, soldiers of the gospel at Greater Light Church and Ministries in Sea-Tac WA., my current church family at Christian Faith Center of Federal Way WA. Thank you to those who have prayed faithfully for me over the years and have honored my ministry.

Special tribute is reserved for my father (Rogers J. Greene Sr.) and Mother (Lula M.C. Greene) who gave me the foundation for ministry through Sunday school before I could remember attending. I thank my mother who prayed for me when I strayed into the world, and still speaks life into my life. I thank God for my brother

Reggie, his family, my sister Lahoma, and her family.

And most of all, I want to thank God for the light that is my wife. Thank you Metesa for allowing me endless hours to write what God purposed for his body. I love you.

Love,

Rogers

The entrance of thy words giveth light; it giveth understanding unto the simple.
Psalm 119:130

OIL FOR LIGHT

Oil for your lamps, Oil for your lamps
Spirit candle of the Lord
Oil trimmed lamp glows
Weighty, warm, and full

Oil for your lamps, Oil for your lamps
Healing wounded soldiers
Broken-hearted burdens
For light, for hope, for journey

Oil for your lamps, Oil for your lamps
Anointed healing balm
When spirit groans
Like fire burning in our bones

Oil for your lamps, Oil for your lamps
Burning brightly real
As ten wise virgins pure
The Glory of God revealed

Original poem by Rogers J. Greene Jr.

And thou shalt command the children of Israel, that they bring thee pure olive oil beaten for the light, to cause the lamp to burn always. (Exodus 27:20)

Contents

Chapter 1
Heart Pages 70 times 7 **20**

Chapter 2
Salvation Pages My Light and Salvation **68**

Chapter 3
Faith Pages Now Faith is **116**

Chapter 4
Giving Pages Pressed down and Poured out **150**

Chapter 5
Purpose Pages Prove it! **180**

Preface

Distilling the word of God in the essence of hope, faith and love, **Pages of Light** is fresh oil for your life and ministry. It is an anointed compilation of wisdom and revelation in the knowledge of God. It is the record of a developing dialogue with God's word that is divinely practical. This reading is designed to ignite your spiritual life and burn brightly into your daily living. It will facilitate and develop an anointing for living and energize your life with light for every decision and daily circumstance. Therefore, read it with your spirit not only your natural eyes. In doing so, It will transport and transform your thinking and set a course for discourse with the mysteries of God.

In the end, my hope is that you will read sections of this book repeatedly. That you will engage this book as you would a fountain, drinking often and as deeply as you require, fulfilling your deepest spiritual desire. May **Pages of Light** illuminate your way along your personal pilgrimage, igniting your spirit, restoring your soul, and making you whole.

Introduction

In Chapter 1, **70 times 7**, we explore the truth that your heart is the epicenter of your life. All of success in life depends on the condition of your heart. In truth, everything you are and hope to become is vitally dependent upon your heart, its condition and the desires of your heart. It is certain that if you cannot get your heart right; you will not get your life right. We explore the conditions of the heart that represent brokenness and solutions for healing these emotional and spiritual ailments. *If the light that is in thee be darkness, how great is that darkness! (Matthew 6:23).*

How you see what you see in life and your appetites are at the core of your being dictating every aspect of your living. This section may be blinding at first then warm and healing. Featured topics include: **Covenant over Cosmetics, Crime Dramas, The Shame and Blame Game** and **Crowns for the Crippled.**

In Chapter 2, **My Light and Salvation,** we explore the truth that to begin the restoration of your heart you must be born again or saved. In this section we reflect on the importance of being saved. In addition, we find a blueprint for those who *are* saved and *ready to give an answer for the hope they have in God. (I Peter 3:15)* This section will prepare you to be an effective witness of Jesus and properly share salvation.

Many are saved but unaware of what happened when they were saved. This section details what grace afforded and love consummated through Jesus our Savior that you might be saved, sanctified, and filled with the Holy Ghost. Featured topics include: **What Must I Do to Be Saved? Naked and Not Ashamed, Amazing Grace!** and **Friends of God.**

In Chapter 3, **Faith: Now faith is...** provides some deeper revelation regarding the elements of faith. We know that *the just shall live by faith. (Romans 1:17)* At first glance faith may appear only passive. By further inspection we discover that faith is both active and passive. One who really believes will act on his belief. Biblically stated, *faith without works is dead. (James 2:17)* Hereafter, you will view faith as not only waiting but initiating, dominating, and creating what you will. You were created to create and dominate your world by faith. Featured topics include: **Faith Has Taught us Faith, Don't Feel it! Faith It! Teach Your Tongue,** and **Living Without a Doubt.**

In Chapter 4, **Giving: Pressed Down and Poured Out,** we explore the thought that giving is living. Now that your heart has been prepared through forgiveness, being forgiven, and faith, we now explore giving. At this point in the reading you will realize the importance of getting your heart healed and whole. All of your living depends on your giving. However, if you are not whole or too hurt you will withhold and not give. If you have not practiced forgiveness, stop at this point and return to the heart pages. Hopefully you are now free to give as Jesus gave. Upon completion of this section you will be a conduit of the blessings of God and able to create an eternal flow in your life that overflows into the lives of others. From this point you will begin to prosper in an unprecedented way. Featured topics include: **The Tithe:**

Divine Dimes, Two Mites are More, We Have This Treasure, and **What's Love Got To Do with Giving?**

In Chapter 5, **Purpose: Prove it!** We examine purpose as the eternal word that God intended for you to embody and present to the world for His glory. Now that giving is a priority in your life, you can focus on purpose. God purposed you before you were born to complete an assignment you were called to earth to fulfill. Of all your giving, your purpose is primary. Just as Jesus came to earth and gave His best, you are called to give your eternal best for God and others. In this section you will interpret the purpose you're pregnant with and begin to give birth to purpose in the world with great success. Featured topics include: **What of Your Dreams? The Power of Rejection, Young Dreamers on the Honor Roll,** and **Live Bigger: Pivot on Purpose!**

Thanks for allowing Pages of Light to fill the pages of your life.

Before we get started, make this confession:

But my horn shalt thou exalt like the horn of an unicorn: I shall be anointed with fresh oil. (Psalm 92:10)

HEART PAGES

Keep Your Heart Diligently

Chapter 1

70 times 7

Then came Peter to him, and said, Lord, how oft shall my brother sin against me, and I forgive him? Till seven times? Jesus saith unto him, I say no unto thee, Until seven times: but, Until seventy times seven. (Matthew 18:21, 22)

Keep thy heart with all diligence; for out of it are the issues of life. (Proverbs 4:23)

How can broken hearts live whole lives? Ultimately, not only does God want to get things to you; He wants to get things through you. This requires a heart whole enough to be the conduit of the blessings of God. At the core of who you are is your heart. Your heart consists of your soul and spirit. Everything you are and everything you do is produced out of your heart. Your whole life flows out of the center of your being. Well, how do you keep your heart, preserve it, and protect it? The word of God is *able to save your soul. (James 1:21)* The word of God sets your heart in godly order and positions you to conceive and produce in a godly manner.

Remember David, who was *a man after God's*

own heart? (I Samuel 13:13, 14) Hold up, wait a minute!
How could David be a man after God's heart when he slept with Bathsheba and later had her husband Uriah killed to cover the matter? (2 Samuel 11)

Remember: All have sinned and fallen short of the glory of God
(Romans 3:23)

David was still considered a man after God's heart because after his initial denial of his sin, he sought God rather than hide from him. Unfortunately, many of you will hide in the garden of disobedience rather than seek God. It is a flaw from Genesis that we run from God rather than to Him when we have sinned. Listen, God says:

My sacrifice [the sacrifice acceptable] to God is a broken spirit; a broken and a contrite heart [broken down with sorrow for sin and humbly and thoroughly penitent] such, O God, You will not despise. (Psalm 51:17 Amplified)

These are the words of David after he sinned against God. In spite of his unworthiness and brokenness, he still sought God. We must seek God in our brokenness to be blessed. We must seek Him beyond the infractions we have committed and those committed against us. With diligence we must seek not to conceal but be healed and become whole in our hearts. Why? Because *Out of it, (the heart) proceeds the issues of life. (Proverbs 4:23)*

Think On These Things

God is willing and able to forgive our sins. Are you willing to forgive yourself and others? The matter of forgiving ourselves is often overlooked as we focus on finding forgiveness for others. However, many are incapacitated by the persistent thoughts of their own inadequacies and sin. Present yourself on the altar of God with all your flaws and give yourself a break. It is *by grace through faith* that we are perfected in God. Let God *perfect that which concerns you.*

What you did may have been stupid and inconsiderate; can you forgive and forget it? We are called to forgive our debtors as God forgave us-that includes forgiving ourselves. By the way, if you cannot forget it (the debt of others against you); you probably have not forgiven it.

What are you willing to forgive that you might live? We are called to intimate relationships with God and man. However, a broken heart resists and rejects intimacy without which there can be no fruit borne in your life. God desires fruit from your life.

Now Pray: Lord forgive me as I forgive those who trespass against me. Lord grant me the grace to forgive myself. Let not a **root of bitterness** *take root in my heart and infect me, leaving me barren and defiled.*

Exercise foresight and be on the watch to look [after one another], to see that no one falls back from and fails to secure God's grace (His unmerited favor and spiritual blessing), in order that no root of resentment (rancor, bitterness, or hatred) shoots forth and causes trouble and bitter torment, and the many become contaminated and defiled by it. (Hebrews 12:15 Amplified)

Reflection 1: Can you afford bitter ruminations over past injustices? Allow the Spirit of God to speak to you concerning this and then record His instructions. You cannot bear fruit with a resentful root in your heart and many vices spring up due to unforgiveness. *The wicked desireth the net of evil men: but the root of the righteous yieldeth fruit. (Proverbs 12:12)*

Perhaps one of the most difficult things to do in life is keep your heart at peace not at war.

Crime Dramas

Woe unto the world because of offences! For it must needs be that offences come; but woe to that man by whom the offences cometh! (Matthew 18:7)

The word of God encourages us that offenses will come but we must not be offended. Who has not been offended? Who has not had someone step precisely on their feelings? It is one thing for offenses to come; it is another to live perpetually in offenses. When you live offended you become defensive in your approach to life and people. And if you live offended, are you really living? In this state, you are no longer building dreams but well reasoned cases against old offenses and potential future offenses. In other words, your heart is not right in you. Your heart becomes small and narrow and God cannot flow His will through you. And God knows that if you live offended you will never finish your purpose.

Likewise, the enemy of your soul knows that if you cannot give you will not live. He knows if you cannot forgive you will not build the dream in your heart. **If you are fearful then you will not be fruitful in life.** If you live in fear your life will not reap fruit, results or glory to God. It will die prematurely like the fig tree in the gospel of Mark and you will have leaves but no fruit. You will be positioned on purpose but not productive. Your purpose will be poisoned by the past. Decide today that you cannot afford to be a fig tree with a show of prosperity but offended to the point of disease and dysfunction.

Think On These Thing

Small hearts don't build big dreams because they quit dreaming. Say like Joseph:

But as for you, ye thought evil against me; but God meant it unto good, to bring to pass, as it is this day, to save much people alive. (Genesis 50:19)

Do you know that what you go through is not just for you? It's also for a myriad of people like you. It's not to "make you strong" as some suggest. It happens on purpose that you might fulfill purpose and deliver others as you were delivered. It's easy to think only of yourself when you endure hardships. But like Joseph we are positioned by pain to help others overcome painful experiences. Like Joseph, your family needs you to hold the bag of money, influence, and deliverance that represents the provision that will save them. If you are offended by them you will not seek their salvation. If Joseph had remained offended by his brother's actions he would have hurt them rather than restore them.

Now Pray: I release my offenders and the offenses held in my heart. God forgive them and forgive me for those I have offended and those I have judged. And of all, I forgive myself as my chief offender. In Jesus name, amen!

Reflection 2: Write the name(s) of your chief offenders; put them on the stand of justice and one by one release the offenders and their offenses. You can't afford the hurt you harbor. It's killing the dream within you!

Covenant over Cosmetics

A man that hath friends must show himself friendly: and there is a friend that sticks closer than a brother. (Proverbs 18:24)

Too often the choice to live in isolation is really an attempt at insulation. Notice this is a choice. Often people need insulation from being hurt again, a painful past, and relationships that failed and continue to cause pain. Many people choose isolation as insulation against many things and many people. It is a deceptive path. The truth is: No one can thrive, only die in isolation. The only appropriate place to hide is in the presence of God. By the way, if the past calls refuse to answer and go on living.

We have all been hurt: but what is isolation costing you? What is it costing you to live a cosmetic life as opposed to a covenant rich life? No one is denying what THEY did to you. However, you will only find wholeness through healing by forgiveness. Give for what they did to you, not what they deserve but what they need. God forgave us through Jesus. He for-gave. Or saying this in reverse, He gave-for what we had done not what we earned but what we needed. That is a measure of His mercy and grace.

> *For God so loved the world, that he gave his only begotten Son, that whosoever believeth in him should not perish, but have everlasting life. (John 3:16)*

Think On These Things

Are you dying to live? You can't live what you are unwilling to forgive. Perhaps you don't have friends or the ones you have are not intimate relationships. This is probably because your wounds are deep and defining your past and present relationships. Perhaps others can't get close to you because close is not comfortable and intimidating. Intimidation is no substitute for Intimacy. Undoubtedly, it is difficult to trust through trauma but trust you must to engage in meaningful life exchanges. We call this love. But you say:

> *...I am poor and needy, and my heart is wounded within me.*

(Psalm 109:22)

To say it bluntly, you must forgive IT to live beyond IT! You cannot afford to live defeated on the battlefield of your mind, accusing and excusing faults and flaws.

> *Now Pray: Lord, help me to the healing I need to engage you and others in intimate godly relationships. Bring people into my life that will help me heal and then I shall come forth as pure gold.*

Reflection 3: Ask yourself, what friendships am I forfeiting because of my need to live protected? How many good relationships have I ruined? Who are my real friends?

Your real friends are those who tell you the truth. They are the ones who identify the boogers in your life. Unfortunately, you will reject these people if you are guarded and defensive with your emotional history. By doing so, you will reject real friends. Ask yourself further: How many present and future friendships are in jeopardy over my heart defects? Determine that you are no longer willing to sabotage relationships and commit to growing strong ones in the future.

Shame and Blame Game

The heart is deceitful above all things, and desperately wicked: who can know it? (Jeremiah 17:9)

It's been said, the truth is hard to find. Is that

really true? Not really. But who will indulge the painful process of examining one's own heart to find it? It's probably easier to play the shame and blame game. In other words, blame other things and other people for one's own deficits and dysfunction. You can never become whole while placing blame. This is worth repeating: You can never become whole while placing blame.

And ye shall know the truth, and the truth, shall make you free. (John 8:32)

You shall know what? You shall know the truth. Not your truth, but THE truth. What happened in the past may be a fact but not the truth. Often past hurts become violations in our hearts which become laws in our lives. Laws are legally binding and dictate our lives from that point backward. We need the truth about ourselves not the facts. These laws impressed by past grievances are lies because they're not what God says about us.

Then, what is the truth? *Thy word is truth (John 17:17)*. God wants to liberate you through His word. It is His words not your own that will make you free. It is interesting that the scripture says, *and ye shall know the truth, and the truth shall* **make you free.** This means the word of God recreates your being to liberate you from your laws. You are liberated by God's word from your laws which are lies dictating your life. *I find a law, that, when I would do good, evil is present with me. (Romans 7:21)*

These laws enacted by past hurts and sin, stand refuting God's order which is God's word. They introduce disorder into your life just as disobedience did to Adam and Eve when they obeyed the serpent's words. Notice that you must obey a lie to live by it. It's not until you obey that you bow.

You must pray that God will test you and discover whether there is any wicked way in you, which would be anything off course with His eternal way and purpose for you. Otherwise, you are bound to avoid the truth and live a lie. Building a life on falsehood will keep you from the eternity in your heart which is your purpose. Inevitably, if you are not healed you will build a wall of shame and blame and deny God's highest and most for your life.

The hardest thing to overcome is one's self-induced truth. It pierces the heart and clogs its arteries from receiving the truth of God and His blood. Can you live the truth?

This is not said to bring condemnation to you. *There is now therefore now no condemnation to them that are in Christ Jesus, who walk not after the flesh, but after the Spirit. (Romans 8:1)* However, you must adopt the Spirit of truth in your heart. And by the Spirit of truth, which is the Spirit of God's word, you will conceive the truth and it will create freedom in your heart. Then you will no longer be obligated to live by what mom or dad said when you were young. You can discard guilt and shame along with personal attacks on your being. God's word *makes* you free.

Think On These Things

You cannot function in dysfunction; you must

allow the word of God to make you more than functional. You must be an overcomer in life not overcome by life.

Too often we confuse who we ARE with what we DO and have done. This compromises our identity. And, if you don't know who you are, you can't get where you're going. Therefore, if we DO something bad, we believe we ARE bad and if we DO well we believe we ARE good. Paul said,

But by the grace of God I am what I am: and this grace which bestowed upon me was not in vain; but laboured more abundantly than they all: yet not I, but the grace of God which was with me.
(I Corinthians 15:10)

Who hath bewitched you? (Galatians 3:1) You will never be good enough to be good enough. And trying to overcome the words of those who said you were not good, is a futile exercise leading to more dysfunction and groveling attempts to gain acceptance from others. **Don't discard the best in you because of the rest of you.** God loves you unconditionally. You should love yourself the same and allow the grace of God to transform you.

Now Pray: Lord, examine me, and see if there is any wicked way in me and lead me in the way everlasting. Create in me a clean heart, O God; and renew a right spirit within me. (Psalm 51:10)

Reflection 4: To be deceived we must choose to believe a lie. The devil cannot blind you without your choice to be blinded. We must choose darkness in order to be blinded to the truth. After reading this section record the lies you have lived by. What did THEY say about you that God never said? What have you come to believe is true and insurmountable regarding *who you are* and capable of being? Write these in pencil then erase them both literally and symbolically.

Love Covers

Bless them that curse you, and pray for them which despitefully use you. (Luke 6:28)

  This passage of scripture and the surrounding passages indicate that we can do something about offenses. It indicates that we can love and turn our cheek to be smitten when others violate us. If Jesus said we could, and did it himself, apparently we can forgive the most grievous acts perpetrated against us.

  And as ye would that men should do to you, do ye also to them likewise. (Luke 6:31)

  What you do to others you essentially do to yourself. And, what you refuse to forgive, after all, will keep your heart small. Remember that you have and maintain the capacity to hurt others yourself. It is not only what others have done against you but what you have inflicted on them as well. This thought will allow you to extend grace and mercy to others as needed.

Think of your heart as an eternal account. When others take from you it demands a withdrawal from your account. If you don't forgive you will eventual go bankrupt of love. Forgiveness replenishes the account. Since the nature of your heart is eternal, you may give or forgive without limits. When Peter asked Jesus how often he should forgive his brother; he was looking for a limit. Love has no limits. It knows no boundaries and like the FDIC (Federal Deposit Insurance Corporation) that covers bank deposits, it covers all deposits and withdrawals from the heart's account. Again, love covers all.

Think On These Things

Search if you must, but you will not find a limit in love. What if they slap me? What if they spit on me? What if they pierce me in my side? What if they mock me with a crown of thorns and scorn?

Remember the word that I said unto you, The servant is not greater than his Lord. If they persecuted me, they will also persecute you... (John 15:20)

Reflection 5: If you are presently dealing with a difficult relationship, forgive them and then begin to pray for them. You will find that God will interject himself into the situation and promote you after all. When you love those that hate you, they become the opponents of God not you. And who can fight God and win?

> *But I say unto you, Love your enemies, bless them that curse you, do good to them that hate you, and pray for them which despitefully use you, and persecute you; that ye may be the children of your Father which is in heaven: for he maketh the sun to rise on the evil and on the good, and sendeth rain on the just and on the unjust. For if ye love them which love you, what reward have ye? Do not even the publicans the same? (Luke 5:44-46)*

Anyone can love those who love them; can you love those who seem unlovable? Take the time to record reasons why you *can* forgive and forget why you cannot.

Grace is Granted

And he said unto me, My grace is sufficient for thee: for my strength is made perfect in weakness. (2 Corinthians 12:9)

Often times we are so damaged by sin and subsequent hurts that our conscience is *accusing or else excusing us* and others. We are often looking for the cause of things and why things went wrong while seeking to absolve ourselves of guilt. Can we do this justly? Are we fit for judging ourselves and others? There is a story in (John 9:1-3) of a young man blinded from birth,

> *And his disciples asked him, saying, Master, who did sin, this man, or his parents, that he was born blind? Jesus answered, Neither hath this man sinned, nor his*

parents: but that the works of God should be made manifest in him.

Like the disciples, we assume if something is wrong then someone *did* something wrong. Here Jesus says circumstances are serving a higher purpose; it is for His glory. Of course, not every adverse circumstance is serving God's purpose. The point is we are often looking to make things right and expecting the worst. Are you expecting something to go right or wrong in your life?

Similarly, when we assume something is wrong, we fight to make it right. However, we can't get right without God. This requires His grace.

In addition, we often experience a feud of conscience which involves unspoken questions like: Who's right? Who's wrong? They're wrong and I'm right. This exercise is too weighty for the soul and spirit and often causes a cycle of anxiety. Anxiety is an anchor that builds and will keep you grounded to mediocre living. It sabotages the best in you as well as the God and good in you. Not only is it weighty but unnecessary and eventually you lose your integrity of being. A loss of integrity develops into a lack intimacy and eventual barrenness.

To cover this fight to be right, many people become busy not blessed, timid not triumphant and their lives fold. What is the remedy? *Do not frustrate the grace of God. (Galatians 2:21)*

Grace can do exceedingly more than you ever have or will do. Granted, the work of conscience, the seat of judgments, is to constantly evaluate and make value judgments about people, times and appearances. Whether aware of it or not, we are constantly weighing the good, the bad, and the ugly in ourselves and others. We are amateur sleuths looking for clues regarding right and wrong. We have a series of "who did it?" features playing in the theater of our minds with perfect recall and vivid projections.

In this great production, worthy of an academy award, we are entertaining our greatest fear-that we are bad, wrong, or have been wronged. It is the futile fight is to be right. The problem with this production is that if we are to be declared not guilty, then someone else has to be guilty. We must necessarily make someone else "the accused" to liberate ourselves. We must point the finger and accept no fault.

By pursuing this complex theme, we become in a sense, bone collectors, constantly weighing evidence, presenting condemning evidence from our past, present and future. All this forensic analysis is caused by our fallen humanity and it devastates relationships, and only waste time, effort, energy and emotional well-being.

Many people are doing what they are doing to be right. Many people are working hard, neglecting time with family or drinking excessively to cover their conscience or to be accepted. What are you trying to prove? And *where are thine accusers? (John 8:10)* God's righteousness is the only right, the rest is all wrong.

And be found in him, not having mine own righteousness, which is of the law, but that which is through the faith of Christ, the righteousness which is of God by faith. (Philippians 3:9)

We must be *made* the righteousness of God in Christ Jesus. Because He is righteous we are made right in acceptance of who He is. Further His blood absolves us of all guilt and shame. Did you hear that? His blood shed for you absolves you of guilt when you accept Him as your sacrifice for sin.

How much more shall the blood of Christ, who through the blood of Christ, who through the eternal Spirit offered himself without spot to God, purge your conscience from dead works to serve the living God? (Hebrews 9:14)

Our justice is His grace. Grace is granted, given, and extended not because we deserve it rather because He died for us.

Think On These Things

Do you know the fight against the devil can take on the case for conscience sake? He can become the cause of everything we do or don't do in an attempt to save ourselves. You must declare, "I'm not bad, I'm not good, but I am being perfected". In this mode you don't need to make excuses for "being" because grace is getting you right. Submit yourself to God's all sufficient grace. His grace is enough to complete you.

And such trust have we through Christ to God-ward: Not that we are sufficient of ourselves to think anything as of ourselves; but our sufficiency is of God. (2 Corinthians 3:4, 5)

Now Pray: Lord I thank you that your grace delivers me from the need to be right, get right, and place blame.

Reflection 6: Do you feel judged? It's probably true that no one is really judging you. The truth is most people are thinking about themselves more than they are thinking about you. Most likely, they're too involved in the tedious process of evaluating themselves to be concerned with your defects. Try to arrest yourself judging yourself and others and remember the grace of God covers you and them.

No Condemnation

She said, No man, Lord. And Jesus said unto her, Neither do I condemn thee: go, and sin no more. (John 8:11)

Judgments of self and others subject relationships to impossible expectations. It is difficult to love others when you feel unlovable and they find it difficult to love you too. Since parties in relationships aren't perfect, love must be rendered unconditionally. It's really about acceptance and not placing blame.

You must realize that the real issues are often within you not outside of you or in others. When you judge yourself and others, you lose the power to love powerfully. When you blame you give power to circumstances and the devil himself. To live a great life this conflict of conscience and judgment must be resolved.

Now Pray: Lord, forgive me for attempting to make myself and others right, to bring justice only you can give. I put down my rocks to forgive. Forgive me for excluding your grace in my race through pride. Help me to overcome the pride that only grace and humility can dethrone.

Reflection 7: What would you do, accomplish, give, live and prevail in, if you did not care what others thought of you? Can you get over yourself and live free of self preservation?

Finding Forgiveness

Then said Jesus, Father forgive them; for they know not what they do. (Luke 23:34)

Honestly, in many instances we do not desire forgiveness we prefer revenge. We want to track people down and exact retribution for our hurts, to which God responds: *Vengeance is mine. (Romans 12:19)*

The greatest deficit of hurting people is a lack of intimacy. Broken hearts lack fruit which is the evidence of their lack of wholeness. The lack of healing is evident in the rehearsal of past hurts. "They did what they did" becomes a law and anthem of the heart and something lived by-like a law. The key is to get healed that you might be whole. *Wilt thou be made whole? (John 5:6)*

You must forgive by choice and will not feelings. You will never feel like forgiving. You must say as Jesus said, *"Father forgive them, for they know not what they do." (Luke 23:34)*

To restate it, no one denies that you have been abused, hurt, misused, misunderstood, and abandoned. However, hurts *only* heal when you forgive. After all, they didn't even know who you were; if they had they may not have crucified you. In other words, they would not have assassinated your identity or subjected you to a process unfit for the King or Queen you are. They would not have abused you physically, mentally, and emotionally had they known who you were.

Recall that Jesus died, *the Just for the unjust,* not for what He did but for others. He did not deserve the agonizing death of the cross but He died. And that is the power of salvation revealed through the gospel. And this is the hope we have in the world and for eternity. The story is great because of the cross but greater because He not only died but forgave them who crucified Him. *Father forgive them* must become the new anthem of your heart. You must say like Jesus, "I forgive them for they did not know what they were doing." In reality, they did not know your purpose or your future. Yes they should have known but they did not. They pillaged you which was not love and dishonored your honor. Remember: *Love covers a multitude of sin. (I Peter 4:8)* In other words, the dark distance between you and them is covered by love. Love gives in spite of crimes committed against you. **Love heals the hate that kills.**

Think On These Things

Transform your past by forgiving those who hurt you, persecuted you and despitefully used you. How do I do that you ask? Forgive them by choosing to forgive. What's at stake? Your inner successes lying dormant until the future calls are at stake. Your future depends on your heart; your heart must be healed if you are to be fruitful in your future.

Hurt people live in the past; whole people transform a hurtful past into a great future!

Now Pray: Lord, I forgive those who used, abused, and accused me in life. They are my critics but you are my Christ!

Reflection 8: It's not a matter of whether you can forgive; it's a matter of whether you will forgive. Ever notice at times you are not breathing? When you live in unforgiveness, your emotional breathing is suspended and your emotional ability to exhale compressed. Start breathing through forgiveness. Write today's date in your journal to commemorate the day you started breathing/living again.

The Butterfly Effect

For as he thinketh in his heart; so is he. (Proverbs 23:7)

Recently, a friend shared with me that she thought alcoholism was a disease. It is hard for me to accept this as true. Let's assume a man may change by changing his thoughts and his choices. No doubt many have been impaired and have chosen vices to deal with "life-trauma". However, if by his choice a man may quit drinking; then he can choose not to drink. Then he cannot claim disease. Alcohol can certainly cause a diseased state but it's not the alcohol rather the choice to drink that is the cause of disease in such a case.

The prodigal son in (Luke 15:11-32) left home thereby separating himself from his father and arrived at a place called riotous living. At some point, the best of him was lying in the mud of his mistakes and bad choices. In that state of being he made a life changing choice. He said within himself, "I will", expressing his will, "return and say I am not worthy and be restored to my father's house." His disease was his choice not his unchangeable condition.

Every new beginning starts with a new choice to change. Some will say "I cannot quit"; I cannot change", "I cannot forgive". If you speak this way, you have relinquished your will to a vice and probably call yourself a victim. What if you said: "My father has servants in his house that are eating better than me, and I'm going home!" What if you changed your thinking?

How do we change our thinking? We change our thinking through the word of God- no less.

And be not conformed to this world: but be ye transformed by the renewing of your mind, that ye may prove what is that good, and acceptable, and perfect will of God. (Romans 12:2)

Your thoughts are vital to the condition of your heart. What are you thinking? Or like the prodigal son, what were you thinking?

Will it actually hurt to adopt a new thought? Will it cause too much pain to change your habitual thinking? Will you renew your mind? It *is* your choice.

Think On These Things

Begin to question your habitual thinking in this manner: "Can I really change my life with a choice or a new thought?" "Is it possible I could change my marriage with God's thoughts about marriage?"

Do you *need* money to be happy? Do you *need* to be married to be whole? Are you becoming the person you want to be by your present choices? Your life will change when you decide to change it. And these changes occur as you renew your mind.

Reflection 9: Do you desire victory over vices? The word of God must enter your heart. God's word, is God's order, is God's standard of living. It may seem unreasonable but one thought of God's word may change your spirit, change your being, change your doing and you can begin again!

It's time to fly! However, before you fly, identify some habitual thoughts plaguing your life, keeping you bound to the temporal address of defeated living. Break out of the suffocating cocoon of conflict and stunted spiritual development. Break free of a treacherous heart and begin to fly by faith to your predestination.

Thoughts Make the Man

A good man out of the good treasure of his heart bringeth forth that which is good; and an evil man out of the evil treasure of his heart bringeth forth that which is evil: for of the abundance of the heart his mouth speaketh. (Luke 6:45)

When you open your mouth you reveal who you *really* are. And what you think you will eventually say, *out of the abundance of your heart. (Luke 6:5)* Thoughts are the voice of words unspoken yet heard. Thoughts are words and they are bought. Yes, thoughts are bought. Now, God's voice is God's thoughts directed toward you and you must choose to hear him and obey.

Consider that you cannot live above the level of your thinking. And your way of thinking develops your way of being which is your spiritual constitution or make up. Your way of thinking dictates your way of being and doing. Who you are in your spirit- which is part of your heart, is who you really are. Therefore in order to change your heart and life you must change your thoughts to alter your spirit. Specifically, you must change your dominate thoughts. Your dominate thoughts are becoming you. This is why scripture invites us to meditate on God's word not our worries.

So do not worry or be anxious about tomorrow, for tomorrow will have worries and anxieties of its own. Sufficient for each day is its own trouble. (Matthew 6:34 Amplified)

The word of God must become a staple in your life in order for you to think right thoughts. His word will make you righteous or position you in right standing with God's highest and most for your life. If we read His words; we will know and think His thoughts. If we think like God we will live godly. Those who meditate in His word day and night *shall prosper. (Psalm 1:2, 3)*

God's thoughts will change the spirit of your mind. And God's Spirit is the Spirit of truth efficacious in changing your thought life. By changing thoughts, the goal is to change your way of thinking then your way of being and doing life.

Think On These Things

How can we change our thoughts seeing we are becoming what we think?

Finally brethren, whatsoever things are true, whatsoever things are honest, whatsoever things are just, whatsoever things are pure, whatsoever things are lovely, whatsoever things are of good report; if there be any virtue, and if there by any praise, think on these things. (Philippians 4:9)

What are you thinking about consistently? It is important because what you are thinking you are becoming and what you are becoming is reflected in what you do. What are you mediating on or chewing over and over in your mind and heart?

Some of you are thinking hopeless thoughts. And though thoughts are immaterial unseen things, they find their substance in the material seen world of your life. Like unseen intruders they show themselves in your relationships, they solidify themselves as beliefs and values often contradictory to the word of God. In essence, they become your life. *As a man thinks so is he. (Proverbs 23:7)*

Reflection 10: Indeed, thoughts are bought and sold in the marketplace of ideas. Where are you getting your information for living? Are you soliciting information from the world? From TV? From blogs? From social networks?

The powerful thing about God's word is that it is

not merely information but it is revelation for living. Dedicate yourself to God's word; it will prosper your life.

But he answered and said, It is written, Man shall not live by bread alone, but by every word that proceedeth out of the mouth of God. (Matthew 4:4)

His words are *spirit and life. (John 6:63)* We are not called to live by every word on television, every word out of our own mouth, or every word out of the mouth of popular culture. God's words are bread, life, spirit, and sustenance for every area of your life.

Pick some Psalms, a book of the bible, or the gospels and begin memorizing scripture daily. This will not only increase your database in the word of God but will sharpen your memory. It will be hard to contract Alzheimer's when the word of God is firing in every synapse of your brain and being. Now begin to meditate on scriptures and commit them to memory.

Warring for the Will

Be sober, be vigilant; because your adversary the devil, as a roaring lion, walketh about, seeking whom he may devour. (I Peter 5:8)

The enemy of your soul desires to capture your will by attacking your emotions. If you notice everywhere you live whether this is at home, school, work or other places, there is often someone or something designed to attack you emotionally. The real plot of the enemy is to capture your will knowing whoever controls your will, directs your destiny.

We are indeed emotional beings. Good or bad, emotions move us. Remember Eve was deceived because she entertained the enemies appeal to her will indirectly through her emotions. In other words, she was moved by her emotions which moved her out of the will of God.

And when the woman saw that the tree was good for food, and that it was pleasant to the eyes, and a tree to be desired to make one wise, she took of the fruit thereof, and did eat, and gave also to her husband with her; and he did eat.(Genesis 3:6)

By the way, both Adam and Eve were deceived by the serpent in the garden not only Eve. The point here is that she saw, she desired, and she took. These are words that express the shift in her will directing her outside the will of God by disobedience. And yes her husband followed her. Did he have to? No, he had a will of his own and could have halted the disobedience by his own obedience.

… having in a readiness to avenge all disobedience, when your obedience is fulfilled. (2 Corinthians 10:6)

In the Garden of Eden we saw the first occurrence of a satanic advertisement. Like today, commercial advertisers are constantly bombarding us with appeals to our thoughts intending to capture our will through emotions. They intend to move us to their product and have us buy them.

To emphasize, whatever and whoever controls your will controls your life. Similarly, whatever or whoever directs your will directs your destiny. The serpent in the garden pressed incessantly on the thoughts of Eve to move her emotions to capture her will. Based on her eventual obedience to his words, he redirected the destiny of man.

Likewise, whatever and whomever you obey you become one with or subject to. After the fall of man, man was no longer one with God but one with the words of his enemy and fell from God.

Check your emotions and guard your thoughts because these are inevitably directing your will. *Casting down imaginations and every high thing that exalteth itself. (2 Corinthians 10:5)* By our will we choose life or death.

I call heaven and earth to record this day against you, that I have set before you life and death, blessing and cursing: therefore choose life, that both thou and thy seed may live: (Deuteronomy 30:19)

Think On These Things

The devil will test you by playing spiritual semantics as he did with Eve. He will come to you and say, "Did God really say?" "Did God really say it was wrong to have sex before marriage?" He will subtly suggest, since your wife is not being intimate with you, it's okay to sleep with others. After all, you have needs. He will prod, "Did God really say you couldn't drink; doesn't a little wine do you good as a medicine?" The whole plot is to have you defect out of the will of God then he will use this access to wreak havoc in your life.

Now Pray: Lord, give me your words and make it plain. I choose life, I choose Christ, I choose the peace of God that passes understanding, and I choose light, love, and the will of God for my life, In Jesus name, amen.

Reflection 11: What is God saying to you NOW? What has He said that you have not obeyed? It's not enough to have the word of God if you're not obedient to it. *If ye be willing and obedient, ye shall eat the good of the land. (Isaiah 1:19).* Write what God has told you to do recently. There is power in writing things given the devil wants to alter God's word in your life. You need to know verbatim what God has said to you. *Whatsoever he saith unto you, do it. (John 2:5)*

The Pursuit of Peace

Peace I leave with you; my own peace I now give and bequeath to you. Not as the world gives do I give to you. Do not let your hearts be troubled, neither let it be afraid. [Stop allowing yourselves to be agitated and disturbed; and do not permit yourselves to be fearful and intimidated and cowardly and unsettled.] (John 14:27, John 16:33 Amplified)

Many in our world, perhaps you as well, are seeking seemingly illusive peace. You are up all night and working all day, without any relief in your being. This is affecting your relationships and fellowship with God. Your heart is under attack. God has a cathartic remedy. It is *the peace of God that passes all understanding. (Philippians 4:7)*

Ever been tormented by a thought, a memory, or an embarrassing incident? This qualifies as something that unsettles and torments you. Whatever that might be it is robbing you of peace.

What is peace? Peace is a state of being. God gives us peace but *not as the world gives peace I give you peace. (John 14:27)* Peace represents unity and integrity of being and wholeness and unity with the Spirit of God.

How do we live in peace? How do we become one or whole in our being? By the way, when you're whole you not only have peace but power to afford provision.

Peace in this world is indeed illusive. How *does* the world give peace? The world offers drugs, alcohol, sex, and other vices as peace offerings. The truth is no one has ever drunk peace, snorted it, bought it, traded it or had sex and gained it. Our world does believe it can offer it though.

Currently, one of the most successful and profitable industries is the drug industry. We're offered a pill for everything from a yellowish toe nail, products for growing hair and erectile dysfunction. The world wants to sell us peace but it cannot be bought.

In reality, a peaceful person has command of their spirit and Jesus is lord of their lives. He is the leader of their spirit and their peace is in knowing God is God. They are secure in Him. We can't find peace outside of God and fellowship with Him. Apparently there is peace without God but it is *as the world gives it.* As such it is not peace but a ploy for money and hopeless imitations.

There are a myriad of disorders in the world and they all involve a separation from one's self which is usually a symptom of being separated from God. Now lets be real, many Christians as well as non Christians are suffering from disorders and personality conflicts. This is so because they have failed at some juncture to turn compartments of their lives over to God and their spirit has been compromised.

The Fight for Right

As mentioned previously, the fight to be right compromises peace. This means the fight to get right or be right without God. We all know people who need to be right all the time. That behavior is a symptom of a broken heart. The fight to be right is the pursuit of self-righteousness by way of self preservation. Often we seek to be right without being justified by God. All this does is force us to look away from our deep flaws and cover them by any means necessary. This is a peace stealer. Imagine how much peace you lose trying to justify everything all the time to save yourself.

Think On These Things

Separate yourself from the thoughts, actions, attitudes, and habits of thought that rob you of peace. Find a harp in God's presence and abide there until all you know is unity in your being. *Seek peace; pursue it!*

Thou wilt keep him in perfect peace, whose mind is stayed on thee: because he trusteth in thee. (Isaiah 26:3)

Now Pray: Lord Jesus, your word says that you are not the author of confusion but peace. I choose peace; the peace of God that passes understanding. I choose you and position myself in your presence. Repeat this until peace is pervasive and presiding in your heart.

Reflection 12: What confusion and disorder can exist in the sea calming peace of God? Identify the peace stealers in your life and lose them in the presence of God. Saul found peace in God's presence when David played upon the harp. **We must find peace in the God of peace.** This is our power position. This is the state of being that results in being properly positioned in God's presence. Order your thoughts and ideas, limit your focus to His person and all clouds of doubt and fear will cease. Write your peace stealers and crush them like the cheap imitations they are. Write them then erase them from your mind literally and symbolically.

Cluttered Hearts

As the deer pants for the water brooks, so panteth my soul after thee, O God. My soul thirsteth for God, for the living God: when shall I come and appear before God? (Psalm 42:1, 2)

When the heart of a man is free; he invariably seeks the heart of God.
Life is filled with distractions and blinding turbulence making it difficult for us to embrace holy abandonment in the presence of God. This means to seek God with *the whole heart* as one might seek water with thirst. A cluttered life does not afford this true seeking of God *only*. The problem many have is they rarely find sacred moments to seek God like David did. It is difficult if not impossible between soccer practice, jobs, movie

going, television viewing and many other mundane activities to find God. You might say David would have been hindered in his pursuit of God too with these demands on time.

The question is: Do you want God more? Do you want him more than memories, worry, anxiety, pain, suffering, jobs, and entertainment?

So when they had dined, Jesus saith to Simon Peter, Simon, son of Jonas, lovest thou me more than these? (John 21:15)

The question proposed to Peter was not whether he loved Jesus but did he love Him *more than these?* Peter at this juncture had spent time with Jesus and had earlier denied Him. Here Jesus seeks to restore him for the ministry he was called to. The question is the same for you. Do you love God more? You may know Him on some level and visited His presence on occasion, but do you love Him more? Is there a competing idol in your heart? Who or what rivals God in your life? Here's a test: Do you seek God only in a crisis or do you seek Him at all times? Your heart will tell you it is faithful but God will prove your heart for you. You must reduce your one desire to one, God who is one.

One thing have I desired of the Lord, that will I seek after; that I may dwell in the house of the Lord all the days of my life, to behold the beauty of the Lord, and to enquire in his temple. (Psalm 27:4)

And

O magnify the Lord with me, let us exalt his name

together. (Psalm 34:3)

Man is a magnifier. His soul enlarges things and persons, which can be good and bad. Have you magnified God above your present circumstances? Have you magnified or made God bigger than worry and fear? *But Sanctify the Lord in your hearts. (I Peter 3:15)*

The biggest thing in your life becomes your life. We often magnify our mistakes more than our miracles. God must be honored above all devotions. *Christ who is our life. (Colossians 3:4)* We must practice total abandonment. This is the only cure for our cluttered hearts and double mindedness.

Can you leave the world of noise and busyness; can you find refuge in Him? Can you seek the face of God with your heart full of desire for Him? *I will say of the Lord, He is my refuge and my fortress: my God; in him will I trust. (Psalm 91:2)*

It's our challenge to live in the world yet not of the world. We cannot find God in the clamor of circumstances and the bustle of anxious living. He is too holy and honorable to be found in less intimate times.

Be still and know that I am God: I will be exalted among the heathen; I will be exalted in the earth. (Psalm 46:10)

Think On These Things

Have you desired an escape from this world? Get quiet. While the dew is still on the roses, tell Him all about your trouble. *In his presence is fullness of Joy*, peace, love, and everything we need.

Clutter in our lives shades the face of God; we then lose His presence and in doing so we lose our singular focus on Him and the power to live like God.

Now Pray: Lord, help me to escape the world in your presence each day. This is the generation that seeks him; they that seek his face. (Psalm 24:6)

Reflection 13: At the end of each day, ask yourself, did I seek God with singular focus or did I allow the clutter of the day to shade my savior's face, mute His voice and shield His beauty? List the frequent distractions you experience and find a scripture to combat each one. Later in Volume 2 of Pages of Light we will discuss practicing the presence of God and that will help too. Remember we capture God with our whole heart and nothing less is sufficient to find God.

Overcoming Anxiety and Depression

Do not fret or have any anxiety about anything, but in every circumstance and in everything, by prayer and petition (definite request), with thanksgiving, continue to make your wants known to God. (Philippians 4:6 Amplified)

This section is devoted to overcoming anxiety and depression. The scripture above basically states that if you pray then you don't have to worry and simply *make your wants known* to God. It does not say needs but wants. Isn't it true that the things we desire are often wants not needs? We want what others have so our budget is unbalanced with all the things we *want*. This causes anxiety and we forget to pray. God says simply make your request known and then you do not need to worry.

Remember Elijah in the wilderness wishing to die?

> *But he himself went a day's journey into the wilderness, and came and sat down under a juniper tree: and he requested for himself that he might die; and said, It is enough; now, O Lord, take away my life; for I am not better than my fathers. (I Kings 18:46)*

This passage of scripture gives us some keys to unlock the door of depression.

1. Seek fellowship over fatigue. Elijah is alone and tired. After being used by God he is fatigued and in that state loses the vitality of his victory. It is true that sometimes we are just tired and want relief from life's persistent demands. Some leaders are ready to give up their ministry not because they have no vision, but because they are simply tired and *feel* alone. Don't die because you're tired. Don't give up because you feel alone.

2. Stop competing and comparing. While tired and feeling alone, Elijah started competing and comparing himself to others. He compared himself to others and thereby depreciated and depressed his self worth. Many of you are competing and comparing yourself to others and depressed because you value them more. Notice that when you're depressed nothing satisfies. Nothing you do is good enough and your victories are short lived. How could this great prophet of God be depressed? He was tired and feeling alone while competing and comparing. Not only that, his way of thinking became his way of being-depressed. *Note: After some of your greatest feats in the Spirit, you will find your hardest test of faith.*

3. Seek fellowship with God. Elijah lost fellowship with God thereby he lost his power to prevail over and became overwhelmed within his own heart. Overwhelm means:

To cover over completely, as by a great wave; to submerge; hence, to overpower; crush.

If you're not careful great waves of thought will submerge you, cover, overpower you and eventually crush you. Where does all this start? It starts in the mind of man.

What you must know is that depression is disguised as the spirit of depression developed and cultivated through your thinking. It will eventually overwhelm you and overpower your whole mind, body, and spirit if you don't change your thinking.

As a spirit, the spirit of depression gives you the ability to be depressed. This is why some feel they have no control over depression. The spirit of depression allows you to be depressed and becomes part of who you are and therefore you feel you have no power over it.

Think On These Things

Why is it that we accept ourselves a certain way

and surmise we cannot change? How can we overcome depression?

And as he lay and slept under a juniper tree, behold, then an angel touched him, and said unto him, Arise and eat. (I Kings 19:4)

Like Elijah, depression can be overcome as we return to fellowship (Arise and eat) with God. This changes our thoughts and our spirit for deliverance. Either by invitation or by submitting to God's word and presence, we can change the spirit of our minds.

To be delivered from depression you must change the spirit of your mind or your way of thinking. In addition you may express your will. You may say, "I choose to be free from anxiety and depression." Expressing your will promotes your spirit above the spirit of depression and positions your spirit to receive what it needs.

Emotional weight can be overcome with the weight of God's word, which is His truth. God's glory is weightier or greater than the weight of depression. This means it has the power to crush the spirit trying to crush you. It can overwhelm overwhelming and deliver you whole. Therefore take authority over depression and speak the truth of God's word when you feel depressed.

For the word of God is quick and powerful, and sharper than any two edged sword, piercing even to the dividing asunder of soul and spirit, and of the joints and marrow, and is a discerner of the thoughts and intents of the heart. (Hebrews 4:12)

However, before you accept a diagnosis of depression, accept the word of God. Allow His word to be the judge and umpire of your heart.

Now Pray: Lord Jesus, deliver me from the spirit of depression and give the oil of Joy for the spirit of heaviness. I confess I am delivered from anxiety and depression and will never be depressed another day in my life, In Jesus name, amen.

Reflection 14: Because of depression, the weight in your soul draws your spirit down and you lose energy for life. Charge your spirit with the words of God. Confess His word and your heart will be energized again. This is a process of learning to think God's thoughts and exercise authority over that depressive spirit. The spirit of anxiety and depression is the spirit of fear. Confess (2 Timothy 1:7) as well as (John 14:1) until your spirit captures God's truth and dispels the lies depression speaks.

Create and Dominate

And God blessed them, and God said unto them, Be fruitful, and multiply, and replenish the earth, and subdue it: and have dominion over the fish of the sea, and over the fowl of the air, and over every living thing that moveth upon the earth. (Genesis 1:28)

Sadly, a common response of those who are hurt and not healed is to control and dominate relationships.

This is a fearful response and in fear man does not create as he was purposed for. He rather multiplies mess, replenishes his arguments, subdues other people not things, and becomes a dictator instead of taking dominion as God intended.

God did not create you to control and manipulate rather to dominate! The idea of emotionally hurt people is that if they can control and manipulate people in relationships then they may prevent further hurts. They assume in their pain that if they control the terms of relationships then they hold power over others and therefore others don't have the power to hurt them- again. It's an endless exhausting exercise of control and manipulation in an attempt to inoculate one from more pain. What if the hurts were healed through forgiveness? Would there be a need for this futile exercise? What might you be free to be and do if you did not have this need to control everything and everyone?

The hurt heart does what Ananias and Sapphira did in (Acts 5:1-11). They kept a portion of the sale of property for themselves. As it relates to the heart they never gave themselves, they gave a selected portion. *Whiles it remain, was it not thine own? (Acts 5:4)* Or still yours? The problem with broken hearts is they can't give all. They are able to give something but not everything. True covenant relationships and giving require you give your whole self, not a portion.

You can do more than control and manipulate; you can dominate! We were created to dominate, be fruitful and multiply. However, God never intended for us to dominate people but purpose, things and the earth.

A whole heart gives wholly and a free heart

creates successful relationships rather than control and manipulate. By the way, no one wants to be controlled or manipulated. And that's why many lack friends.

You are a creator like God not a manipulator. If this isn't you but someone you know; realize they're desperately trying to protect themselves from more pain. The only escape is to be healed of hurts. Those who control and manipulate in relationships are often those who appear to be your friend then at other times they treat you badly or hurt you. Based on the potential to be hurt again, they create this separation to protect their wounded hearts. Unfortunately, they are unable to develop and maintain healthy relationships. There is a part of them they cannot fully disclose. They're hiding their true selves. They are critically wounded and committed to concealing the gapping wound. In the end, they lack integrity in their being; therefore they lack intimacy and consequently they bare no fruit and have no friends. This condition requires, *beauty for ashes; the oil of Joy for the spirit of heaviness. (Isaiah 61:3)*

Think On These Things

If you are too hurt to be whole, you will resort to control. If you are too broken to be blessed, you will resort to stress. Healed over hurt, you'll be both blessed and fruitful. Here's a secret: **Transparency will transform you and relieve you of isolated defensive living.**

Now Pray: Lord I am a creator like you are the creator. Help me to create my world and build godly relationships. May my mouth not release missiles that devastate my relational landscape.

Reflection 15: Am I a relationship killer? Do I dominate people like they are things? Whom have I controlled and need to ask for forgiveness?

No Turning Back

And Jesus said unto him, No man, having put his hand to the plough, and looking back, is fit for the kingdom of God. (Luke 9:62)

The greatest enemy of the future is the past. If you're not careful, a broken heart will bind you to your past. Sometimes the prospects of the future can be so daunting that we wish for the past. We call them the "good old days". The good old days are less threatening because we have lived them already. The future has yet to be proven so we trust it less.

You will know your spirit is not right in you when you have a vision for a defeated past. Looking back is an attack and a symptom of a diseased heart.

Have you spoken to old acquaintances and all they talk about is how you used to party? And often they confess they are still doing the same things 25 years later? Who gets in their car for a road trip and keeps looking back reflecting every mile about the last 50 miles? And if so, is that a way to reach a final destination?

We must be engaged in the future. It is true, that if you value your past more than your brilliant future, you will live in the past without the promise of a future. Now the past isn't all bad but it is no future.

For I know the thoughts I think toward you, saith the Lord, thoughts of peace, and not of evil, to give you an expected end. (Jeremiah 29:11)

God has a great future bearing great fruit for you. You must know the past does not equal the future; the future does not equal the past. By the way, in God there is no past, present, and future only the eternal NOW. This is because, the things that WERE have already been. The things that ARE have been and will be. The things that *will be* ARE and have been. Your future is now! Not yesterday or even tomorrow. Live eternally now!

Think On These Things

Now forgetting those things which are behind we press toward the mark for the prize of the high calling of God in Christ Jesus! (Philippians. 3:13, 14)

You cannot escape your past but you can transform it. Your vision should be the future God has purposed for you. If you fall, fall forward into your destiny!

And we know that all things work together for good to them that love God, to them who are the called according to his purpose. (Romans 8:28)

Now Pray: Lord heal my memories because

sometimes I still recall the memory and in doing so I reclaim the pain.

Reflection 16: Imagine yourself in the present and future free to give, free to live. See yourself going and growing in God, transported, transformed and triumphant. Write three things you will do this year to alter your future and impact the lives of others.

Crowns for the Crippled

And Jonathan, Saul's son, had a son that was lame in his feet. He was five years old when the tidings came of Saul and Jonathan out of Jezreel, and his nurse took him up, and fled: and it came to pass, as she made haste to flee, that he fell, and became lame. (2 Samuel 4:1-7)

 A Crown: Anything which imparts beauty, splendor, honor, or finish; also the high state of quality of anything.
 Mephibosheth [Mu-fib-uh-sheth], whose name means "exterminator of shame" is dropped when he is a baby and left crippled in both feet. Through no choice of his own he is maimed for life.
 In life, we too are often dropped and left for dead. Life is full of content without context leaving many without meaning for the things that happened. They are left disfigured, maimed and undesirable with a confused undefined identity. The innocent are often left without recourse and isolated. Victims go bleeding without a blessing. Too often, we lose our God-given design

through misfortune and mishaps. Problems often overwhelm purpose. People are reduced to problems and disenfranchised. Our honor is cast down and laid in the dust of dysfunction. *Thou hast made void the covenant of thy servant: thou hast profaned his crown by casting it to the ground. (Psalm 89:39)*

How many of you are crippled because of someone else's actions of indifference, maliciousness or negligence. Like Mephibosheth, you were going somewhere to do something and be somebody. But someone abandoned you, abused you, and left you crippled. Not only that, they have never returned to say they were sorry or explain the circumstances under which this tragedy occurred. All you want is an explanation, right? You are crippled for life and they have gone on with their lives. The question is: Is that the end of your life? Is that all you will ever be, a cripple?

Then King David sent, and fetched him out of the house of Machir, the son of Ammiel, from Lodebar. (2 Samuel 9:5)

Lodebar means "without pasture". King David who held the authority to place honor, fetches Mephibosheth out of a place of wandering and wondering. He calls him from a low place to a high place in the King's presence. Honor is bestowed upon the dishonorable. Love is extended to the seemingly unlovable. A place is given to one who has no place, who is powerless and crippled.

God is calling you from the places you have fallen to a high place in His presence, to give you honor. There is no need to remain a cripple without a crown. **God gives crowns to the crippled!** The scars are still there but you're released from the war within. God is replacing your shame with His glory. He is adding to your life a crown of splendor and favor. You may have fallen or they dropped you; but God is lifting you up! *For thou art the glory of their strength: and in thy favor our horn shall be exalted. (Psalm 89:17)*

Think On These Things

And the LORD said unto Joshua, This day have I rolled away the reproach of Egypt from off you. Wherefore the name of the place is called Gilgal unto this day. (Joshua 5:9) God is going to remove the reproach upon you through the blood of Christ.

Gilgal means circle. You're no longer living in circles. God is allowing you to circle back to your original place of honor. Go tell others God has crowns for the crippled!

Remove my reproach, bitterness and shame
Deliver me from the propensity to blame
Though crippled and left behind
You have placed upon me favor and a crown

Reflection 17: *What shall we then say of these things? If God be for us, who can be against us? (Romans 8:31)*

Chapter Notes

_____

_____

_____

_____

We have also a more sure word of prophecy; whereunto ye do well that ye take heed, as unto a light that shineth in a dark place, until the day dawn, and the day star arise in your hearts…(2 Peter 1:19)

SALVATION PAGES

My Light and Salvation

Chapter 2

What Must I Do To Be Saved?

And brought them out, and said, Sirs, what must I do to be saved?
(Acts 16:30)

Many have complicated salvation thinking that some how we may earn what is clearly given to us by God. We *do not frustrate the grace of God* as though there were some way we could earn the gift of salvation. *It is the gift of God.* It is not earned it is received. No effort can earn what God provided and Jesus died for. Scripture clearly states,

For by grace are ye saved through faith; and it is the gift of God. (Ephesians 2:8)

We must ask and others will, what must I do to be saved? Jesus said to Nicodemus, *"Except a man be born of water and of the Spirit, he cannot enter the kingdom of God." (John 3:5)* What? How can a man be born again when he is old? What must you do to be saved?

The short answer is there is nothing you can do to earn salvation because Jesus did it all.

But God commendeth his love toward us, in that

while we were yet sinners, Christ died for us. (Romans 5:8)

Indeed, He who knew no sin died for a world of sinners.

Now to speak of sin and sinners we must revisit the fall of man in the Garden of Eden. The Garden of Eden represented the parameters of the will of God for man. Imagine God was in man and man was in the Garden existing within the will of God.

And the Lord God took the man, and put him into the Garden of Eden to dress it and to keep it. And the Lord God commanded the man, saying, Of every tree of the garden thou mayest freely eat: But of the tree of the knowledge of good and evil, thou shalt not eat of it: for in the day that thou eatest thereof thou shalt surely die. (Genesis 2:15-17)

In the beginning man lived in the context of God's presence with the content of God's likeness. He was created in the image and likeness of God with the context of God's presence as his perpetual dwelling. Man was intended to live vitally connected to God. God never intended for man to live separated from Him.

We may think the Garden of Eden was too restrictive. You may wonder why God would place such a restriction on man and tempt him so. Remember that man was created to be like God, not God. The tree of the knowledge of good and evil (Genesis 2:17) was not set as a temptation but a boundary for man to live in authority under God. This is why the devil in an attempt to usurp the authority of man and his position in submission to God, said to the woman,

Ye shall not surely die, For God doth know that

in the day ye eat thereof, then your eyes shall be opened, and ye shall be as gods, knowing good and evil. (Genesis 3:4, 5)

Man was already a god like God therefore the enemy's real temptation was for man to exceed the will of God by desiring "to be" God. The enemy tempts us to be something we already are or desire things we already have or be what we can never be. If he does not tempt you to exceed God's will he will often tempt you to embellish and exaggerate it.

Then too, we cannot be tempted by what we don't desire.

Let no man say when he is tempted, I am tempted of God: for God can not be tempted with evil, neither tempted he any man. But every man is tempted, when he is drawn away of his own lust, and enticed. (James 1:13, 14)

This tells us that if the desire is not in us then we cannot be tempted by it. If you have no desire for cake, you cannot be tempted by cake. The enemy finds our areas of temptation and seeks to exploit them. Remember, his desire is to direct your will through your appetite out of the will of God. Therefore, be diligent to properly condition your inner appetite. Your appetite is either leading you away from or to the will of God.

The devil tempts the married man to seek in another woman what he already has in his wife. He tempts children to leave the safety of their parents' counsel for the easy words of their friends. He tempts the great pastor of 100 people to seek the prestige and power of 10,000 members and a mega church. For this pastor, 10,000 members are too far outside the will of God and he misses rather than maximizes the potential of his God-given vision. An inch outside the will of God is too far. Don't allow a good thing to replace the God thing in your life.

Think On These Things

Beware that the enemy will nudge you subtly with the promise of success beyond God's will. There is no success beyond God's will and the devil knows it!

Notice too that temptation often occurs within the context of God's will not outside of it. Temptation occurs while you're in the will of God. Temptation is the test to be drawn away and out of the will of God often to something you already possess. For example, many Christians are running to the world for answers. What in the world do you want? Whatever you are seeking outside of God's will, the world and the devil will offer it to you, you must decline.

Therefore, my beloved brethren, be ye steadfast, unmovable, always abounding in the work of the Lord, forasmuch as you know that your labour is not in vain in the Lord. (I Corinthians 15:58)

Whatever, you do, do it in the Lord.

On the other hand, recognize that just because you have been tempted does not mean you have sinned. Many people mistake temptation for participation. Remember Jesus:

For we have not an high priest which cannot be touched with the feeling of our infirmities; but was in all points tempted like as we are, yet without sin. (Hebrews

4:15)

Jesus was tempted yet without sin. To sin you must exceed the boundaries of God's will which is God's word in whatever form He gives it. You may ask, what if I do not know God's will? His word is His will. Whatever God has said to you by His word is His will. What has God said? Your life depends on God's word.

Now Pray: Lord lead me not in temptation but deliver me from evil.

Reflection 18: Your will is the steering wheel of your life. Who or what is driving you? Ask yourself, Am I on course or have I detoured to lesser desires and veered tragically into the lane violations of life?

As long as you are asking these questions you are aligning yourself with God's best. When you no longer question or examine yourself then you are in jeopardy of taking a great fall. **When an individual or ministry loses its ability to view themselves objectively, then they become offensive to God and defensive with men.**

Ask yourself, am I listening to the devil and the voice of the world whispering against God's will? If you listen like Adam and Eve, the whisper may some day become too loud to ignore, and you may succumb to a fatal capitulation of your will. Stop listening to the altered word of God and seal your hearing with *thus saith the Lord.*

Now list the things that have been whispering in your life and deny them access at once. Things like: Am I really saved? Does God really love me? What if I never fulfill my destiny? What if someone finds out who I really am? What if they find out I'm not what I appear to be?

Be Saved

But what saith it? THE WORD IS NIGH THEE, EVEN IN THEY MOUTH, AND IN THY HEART: that is, the word of faith, which we preach; That if thou confess with thy mouth the Lord Jesus, and shalt believe in thine heart that God hath raised him from the dead, thou shalt be saved. (Romans 10:9)

Now we will answer Nicodemus' pressing question. How can one be born again when he is old? What must you do to be born again? Jesus clearly said you must be born again to enter the Kingdom of Heaven. In the book of Acts the bible says,

And they said, Believe on the Lord Jesus Christ, and thou shalt be saved and thy house. (Acts 17:9)

What must you believe to be saved? Jesus and the Apostles preached the word, it was heard, believed, conceived, and salvation was received. What did Nicodemus need to be born again or born of the Spirit and saved? He had to believe the word made flesh, Jesus. How are we saved or born of the Spirit? We *believe in our hearts and confess with our mouth* and confession is made unto salvation. *(Romans 10:9, 10)* Essentially, by believing we conceive like seed salvation manifested by the work of the Spirit. This is why Jesus said you must be born again of water (the word) and the Spirit. Salvation is a matter of becoming one with Jesus and the operation of the Spirit manifesting salvation in the heart of man. *Only believe. (Mark 9:23)*

What you believe you conceive and receive. Your confession is an expression of what you believe. Confessing Jesus as Lord and Savior is to say what God says, that Jesus is Savior. When you believe God is Savior then you become one with Him and conceive in your spirit God's Spirit and you are born again!

Some may say this is too easy. Ask yourself, what can you do more than Jesus already did? Can you afford salvation? Can *any* of us afford salvation? Can we by works or effort, earn it? Then stop working for it and simply receive by faith. Scripture does admonish us to *work out your own salvation (Philippians 2:12).* However, the next verse says,

For it is God which worketh in you both to will and to do of his good pleasure. (Philippians 2:13)

This means you should continue living saved by the same grace that saved you, not to earn salvation. After all, *it is God at work in you,* not you.

You may ask how is it that God can accept you after all you have done. It is not what you have done or can do, but what He did that you could not do-go to the cross! By grace (what God did) are you saved (separated from sin) through faith (what you believe).

Think On These Things

Why does man need a savior? What are we saved from? We are saved from the sin that separated us from God. By dying on the cross, Jesus separated man from sin.

When God said to man that he would *surely die* if he ate of the tree of the knowledge of good and evil, he meant man would be separated from the life of God eternally.

How it must have pained God after the fall of man to be separated from man, His image and His likeness. And so we need a savior to separate us from sin and restore us to fellowship with God.

Now Pray: I believe in my heart and confess with my mouth the Lord Jesus and I am saved.

Reflection 19: Recall your salvation experience. Write in detail what you experienced on your new birth date. Recall this experience as one who was waiting on death row to pay the penalty for sin and Jesus commuted that sentence.

> What a loving savior
> That he would die for me
> What a love so tender
> My sins he cannot remember

Have you resolved the issue? Have you committed to the solution? Have you taken TIME to settle ETERNITY? That is to simple say: ...I believe with my heart and confess with my mouth the Lord Jesus Christ, and I am saved! (Romans 10:9, 10)

Salvation

Fallen in the garden
Dark separated lost
Hiding from the voice
God man once sought

Naked known in sin
Serpent's words obeyed
Eve deceived beguiled
Captured by his wiles

Lamb stained refrained
Manger born king
Salvation given born again
Every guilty sinner man

Calvary's cross blood shed
Remitting sin torn veil
Crown thorns stained brow
Bruised cursed scorned crucified

Savior salvation restoration
Love died arise believer see
Jesus son savior on a tree
Hung, bleed, died, for you and me

-Original poem by Rogers J. Greene Jr.

But he was wounded for our transgressions, he was bruised for our iniquities: the chastisement of our peace was upon him; and with his stripes we are healed. He was oppressed, and he was afflicted, yet he opened not his mouth: he is brought as a lamb to the slaughter, and as a sheep before her shearers is dumb, so he openeth not his mouth. (Isaiah 53: 5, 7)

Be ye baptized

Go ye therefore, and teach all nations, baptizing them in the name of the Father, and of the Son, and of the Holy Ghost. (Matthew 28:19)

Baptism is the emersion and induction of saved ones into the body of Christ. Salvation reunites us with God through Jesus and His Spirit, while baptism is our integration into His body. We are vitally connected to Jesus our head through His body- the church. Some question whether they need to be baptized. Why would you enter fellowship with Jesus the head of the Church, and not His body? Who marries someone's head but not their body? Jesus was baptized to integrate himself into His body and as an example to all believers following. He didn't need to wash away sin by baptism as we do. But He did require the sanctioning of the Spirit of God as validation of who He was for future ministry and as head of the body of Christ. *This is my beloved son in whom I* am well pleased. (Matthew 3:17)* We require the washing away of our sin through baptism and are raised to a new life in Christ.

Therefore we are buried with him by baptism into death: that like as Christ was raised up from the dead by the glory of the Father, even so we also should walk in newness of life. For he that is dead if freed from sin. (Romans 6:4, Col 2:12.) In baptism we die to our old selves and are raised to a new life by the recognition and sanctioning of God as beloved sons.

Think On These Things

Now Pray: Lord Jesus I thank you that I have been inducted into your body by baptism and resurrected to a new life with you. I thank you that I am a part of your glorious church that shall be caught up with you in the air when you return. Most of all, I thank you that old things are passed away and all things have become new in me and I am saved, sanctified, and filled with your precious Holy Spirit, In Jesus' name, Amen.

Reflection 20: Do you lack power in your life, ministry, and walk with God? *Be filled with the Spirit. (Ephesians 5:18)*

Now realize that being filled with the Holy Spirit and baptized in water are not badges of courage or guarantees of entering heaven. The filling of the Holy Ghost and baptism are empowerment to live like God in the world. And now that you are saved and baptized, it is now time to deposit these experiences into the lives of others that they too might *do exploits* for God in the name of Jesus.

...*the people that do know their God shall be strong, and do exploits. (Daniel 11:32)*

Naked and Not Ashamed

And they were both naked, the man and his wife, and were not ashamed. (Genesis 2:25)

So God created man in his own image, in the image of God created he him; male and female created he them. (Genesis 1:27)

This scripture actually records man as both male and female. At this point in the scripture, God is in man, woman is in man and the man and woman are one in God.

Before the fall of man his inner man appeared as such:

Spirit -spirit
Soul
Body

In the illustration above, man's spirit is aligned with or submitted to the Spirit that is God. In this state, he experienced uninterrupted communion with God. This is the state man was created to live in eternally with God.

...*She took of the fruit thereof, and did eat, and gave also unto her husband with her; and he did eat. And the eyes of them both were opened, and they knew that they were naked... (Genesis 3:6, 7)*

After the fall of man his inner man appeared as such:

> Body
> Soul
> spirit

After the fall, man's spirit was out of fellowship with God, subject to his body and soul and diseased by every ungodly infection. He was naked and ashamed. He became a defector and self-conscious rather than God conscious. His existence now had content without context. He was outside of the Garden of Eden and the presence of God. The spirit of fear indicted his actions. They heard God's voice and were afraid. (Genesis 3:10)

Man was never intended to live out of fellowship with God. In such a state he became officially dead by separation from the life of God.

As a result, our whole man needs saving, spirit, soul and body. We find in scripture the spirit of man may be saved or reunited with God's spirit, the soul is being saved, and the body is yet to be saved. When man is saved his spirit is reconciled back to God. The illustration below shows how that occurs.

Man after the fall in relationship to God:

> God is Spirit
> (Separation due to sin)

Body
Soul
spirit

Notice the separation between God and man is formed by the fleshly or carnal part of man-his soul and body.

After salvation man appears like this:

God is Spirit

Reunited with man's born again spirit

Soul

Body

(Refer to the first illustration of man before his fall from God and notice it is the same illustration as this one)

The illustration above portrays man saved or born again. The complication for man after being born again is his soul is still being saved and his corruptible body is yet to be saved. Paul exclaims who shall deliver me from this body of death. The answer appears in (Romans 8:1),
There is therefore now no condemnation to them which are in Christ Jesus, who walk not after the flesh, but after the Spirit.
We live godly as we *put to death the deeds of the body* and follow the leadership of the Spirit. To do so we must be filled with the Spirit of God. If not, we are bound to live carnal Christian lives. This means we appear saved as below but live by the dictates of the body and soul's desires.

God's Spirit

Born again spirit

Soul

Body

Carnally, we are led by our soul and body not the Spirit of God or our born again spirit. This is a carnal state of being.

Have you heard of cursing Christians? A Christian not submitted to God's Spirit can indeed live like they are not saved. These are often caustic Christians who find it difficult to love as Christ loved. Again, *be filled with the Spirit.* In other words, live under the influence of God's Spirit not the dictates of your fleshly carnal nature.

Think On These Things

Is your light on? Are you a professing Christian and truly the light of the world? Or a diminished shadow of a once brilliant salvation?

Let your light so shine before men, that they may see your good works, and glorify your Father which is in heaven. (Matthew 5:16)

More people will come to Jesus because of your example not your words. What is your life communicating? Is your lifestyle telling the world Jesus lives and saves, or is it an indictment against God and His Christ?

> *Now Pray: Lord, thank you for delivering me to be a deliverer. I pray my light so shines among men that they see my good works and glorify you.*

Reflection 21: Are you saved and living for Jesus? Or are you living for yourself? Are you filled with Spirit of God with the evidence of speaking with other tongues? Is what you're *saying* and what you're *being* congruent with your salvation? And remember, salvation is not *really* about salvation but the Savior.

> *The Lord is my light and my salvation... (Psalm 27:1)*

As witnesses of Jesus, most people are not effective because they don't know Him. It's difficult if not impossible to share about someone you don't really know. If this is you, be diligent to know God rather than know of Him.

Make a list of those you will invite to Jesus this week and pray for them before you extend the invitation. And try inviting people to Christ before you invite them to church.

Let your light so shine before men, that they may see your good works, and glorify your Father which is in heaven. (Matthew 5:16)

Amazing Grace!

For God so loved the world, that he gave his only begotten Son, that whosoever believeth in him should not perish, but have everlasting life. (John 3:16)

The nature of Love is to give. Giving is a measure of grace. Grace is defined by giving unconditionally what is granted not earned.

God so loved the World that He gave. He not only gave but He gave His only; He gave His best. We will explore this thought more in the section on giving.

This portion of the writing emphasizes further that we cannot afford the things grace provides. Paul says,

But by the grace of God I am what I am: and his grace which was bestowed upon me was not in vain; but I laboured more abundantly than they all: yet not I, but the grace of God which was with me.
(I Corinthians 15:10)

His grace is sufficient for you. Indeed, **Grace removes the struggle out of striving, the strain out of struggle, the effort out of earning, and the pretense out of performing.** His grace is more than enough to meet your need without sweat, exertion, or human effort. Let grace graduate you into your place of significance and success. You cannot do what only God *can* do by His grace. The success of truly successful people is that they have surrendered to grace's ability to exceed their ability.

Think On These Things

What is your part? Your part is only to believe God in all things. Then all things become possible.

Jesus said unto him, If thou canst believe, all things are possible to him that believeth. (Mark 9:23)

Is your best better than God's all? If there is one way to earn grace, it is to believe in God who grants grace.

Now Pray: Lord I now lean upon your grace to take me to places I have been purposed for. To overcome things I cannot in my own power. To perform temporal and spiritual feats, your grace is sufficient for me!

Reflection 22: Grace will afford you what effort never will. Continue therefore in His grace. What are you fighting for that you should now give over to God's grace? Your children are not going to change until you allow God to change them. Your finances won't change because you're working three jobs. It is God's ability not yours that will cause you to prosper. Just as you could not save yourself from sin, you cannot save yourself from things. It is cliché, but let go and let God! Identify the things you need grace to topple in your life and *lean not to your own understanding. (Proverbs 3:5)*

How is it that God turns your mess into a

message, your mistakes into a ministry, and uses misfits to reach masses of people? It is His amazing grace!

The Juxtaposition of the Cross

If a man would follow me he must take up his cross and follow me. (Matthew 16:24; Luke 9:23)

To associate with Jesus and identify with Him is to identify with the cross. This means to identify with His brutal death burial and resurrection. Paul said,

That I might know him, the power of his resurrection and the fellowship of his sufferings, being made conformable unto his death
(Philippians 3:10)

What does it mean to take up your cross and follow Jesus?

The cross is the cruel instrument upon which Jesus died to separate us from sin, the sin that separated us from God. We are crucified with Him.

I am crucified with Christ: nevertheless I live; yet not I, but Christ liveth in me: and the life which I now live in the flesh I live by the faith of the Son of God, who loved me, and gave himself for me. (Galatians 2:20)

When Jesus died we were separated from sin symbolized by the torn veil in the temple as He died on the cross. (Matthew 27:51) The veil was rent as was His flesh and thereby we gained access to God beyond the veil. By enduring the cross, Jesus tore us away from the power of sin and gave us the power of salvation.

Paul said, *I die daily (I Corinthians 15:31).* This is to say he undressed himself of self and adorned the Spirit of God daily. Jesus asked the disciples in (Matthew 20:22) if they were able to drink of the cup He would drink of and be baptized with the baptism He would be baptized with. *They say unto him, We are able.* And as they were so are we. You too, by the Spirit of God, can suffer in the flesh and die in order to live unto God.

All of this is to say, Christianity will cost you something. It will not only cost you something; it will cost you everything because of the cross. You too must suffer that you might be sanctioned.

If any man come to me, and hate not father, and mother, and wife, and children, and brethren, and sisters, yeah, and his own life also, he cannot be my disciple. (Luke 14:26)

Hate in this scripture means that no other love rivals the love you have for God. It also indicates that you would *so* separate yourself from others and your own self that it is comparable to hate.

It will cost you your reputation and relationships to follow Jesus. That is part of your cross experience. You cannot love God with all and love others more. Similarly, you cannot love God with all without losing self love. Let your love for God loathe self love until He is all you know and love. It will cost you your life to love Jesus this way as you give your life for His.

In truth, the world does not like Jesus; and they don't like you either. In (John 15:22), Jesus says:

If I had not come and spoken unto them, they had not had sin; but now they have no cloak for their sin.

Are you warming yourself with the world? Peter

warmed himself while Jesus was in the process of being delivered up for crucifixion. Subsequently, he denied Him three times refusing to be identified with Him to preserve his own life. This same Peter said to Jesus *though all leave you I will not leave you* and Jesus responded,

Get thee behind me, Satan: thou art an offense unto me: for thou savorest not the things of God, but those that be of men. (Matthew 16:23)

Jesus rebuked Peter's declaration. He did so because Peter's words appeared noble and holy but they were self centered and opposed to Jesus' earthly purpose.

Inevitably, like Peter, what you say you believe will be tested in the crucible of the world. *Are you not one of the disciples?* But fear not, Jesus says, *I have overcome the world. (John 16:33)*

I have given them thy word; and the world hath hated them, because they are not of the world, even as I am not of world. (John 17:14)

You can't follow Christ without embracing the cross of Christ. You cannot embrace the cross without the power to bare the cross by the Holy Spirit. His invitation extends to you: Take up your cross and follow me!

Think On These Things

Remember Peter and the other disciples before the day of Pentecost were unable to wait one hour with Jesus and failed him? In fact, it was not until the day of Pentecost that the disciples were empowered by the descent of the promised Holy Spirit to live for Christ and die for the gospel of Jesus Christ.

And when the day of Pentecost was fully come, they were all with one accord in one place. (Acts 2:1)

The disciples after Pentecost were bold preachers with signs following their ministry.

Today, ask God to fill you with His Spirit with the evidence of speaking in other tongues that you might be a bold witness of Him and able to take up your cross and follow Him.

Now Pray: Lord Jesus, I still cannot fathom the brutality of your crucifixion but I thank you for its blessing.

But God forbid that I should glory, save in the cross of our Lord Jesus Christ, by whom the world is crucified unto me, and I unto the world. (Galatians 6:14)

Reflection 23: What has it cost you to follow Christ? Whatever the cost, Paul says in (Philippians 3:7)

But what things were gain to me, those I counted loss for Christ.

Have you assessed what it will cost you to further follow Christ? In the end, it will cost you everything to follow Jesus but follow on to know Him anyway!

For which of you, intending to build a tower, sitteth not down first, and counteth the cost, whether he have sufficient to finish it? (Luke 14:28)

The cross upon which Jesus died stands juxtaposed to the cross you must bare for Christ. But first the cross must do its sanctifying work or you will remain an unqualified sacrifice unusable in the service of God.

Many people will not come to Jesus because of the friends they will lose or the next party they would miss or the family they will upset. Similarly, religion and traditions keep people from Jesus who saves because of the cross they must bare.

Inevitably, there's a cross for you and there's a cross for me. In your devotional time sift through a hymnal and sing some cross songs until you feel the weight of the cross bearing on your soul in power.

Sinner Save Yourself?

Then said I, Woe is me! For I am undone; because I am a man of unclean lips, and I dwell in the midst of a people of unclean lips: for mine eyes have seen the King, the Lord of hosts. (Isaiah 6:5)

Many people are waiting to rid themselves of sin, habits, and the past, before they come to God and serve Him. If you could do this on your own, you would not need God. There are many examples in scripture of God using imperfect people to perfect His perfect purposes in the earth. You may be asking, "How can God use me?" God can use you because He sees you in ways you do not and cannot see yourself. He knows the real you. He knows you as the one He ordained before you were in your mother's womb. And incredibly, He still loves you. There's something about you that God desires to use for His glory. Yet undone, He desires you. Isaiah exclaimed,

Woe is me for I am undone!

Not finished yet? God will complete you. This is not to lower your esteem or foster guilt but to help you see your need for God's grace. We must present our imperfections. He will send the angel from the altar with fire to purge the altar of your heart.

Then flew one of the seraphims unto me, having a live coal in his hand, which he had taken with tongs from off the altar: And he laid it upon my mouth, and said, Lo, this hath touched thy lips; and thine iniquity is take away, and thy sin purged. (Isaiah 6:6, 7)

Notice it is God's doing to purify us for service, not our own effort to perfection.

Imperfect as you are, God wants to present you to the world. Yes, you! With all of your warts, imperfections, flaws, and scars, He still desires you. He knows you and still loves you perfectly and unconditionally. He wants to use your mouth to speak to masses. He wants to use your leadership ability to lead those masses on a mission. He wants that mission to serve His eternal purpose. And to God be the glory!

Jesus was bruised, wounded, and after His resurrection, He presented himself to His disciples. Thomas put his finger in Jesus' wounds to prove He was resurrected. We too can experience a resurrection.

As a living sacrifice, your wounds are imperfections God can use as a witness of His delivering, resurrection power. There's something in you, something about you, and your imperfections that make you valuable for His purpose. Realize that many have been wounded as you have been. They need to see your scars. They need to know they can go to the cross and back. They need to know they can overcome grave situations and experience a resurrection of their divine purpose. They need to know their wounds are not fatal but fortunate. What is your testimony?

We overcome by the blood of the lamb and the word of our testimony. (Revelations 12:11)

Think On These Things

It is obvious by scripture that God does not use perfect people to perform His will. He would then have no one to use. It must be that He uses imperfect people in a perfect way. But more importantly, God uses prepared people to pursue godly perfection, which is His purpose.

Now Pray: Lord, as imperfect as I am you chose me. I pray my scars help others win their wars. I pray my tears help others overcome their fears. I pray my crosses help others recover their losses. And, in the end, may your sacrifice save lives through me, in Jesus name, amen.

Reflection 24: Have you been hiding your scars? We need to hear your testimony of deliverance. Don't allow the enemy to steal your testimony. If he steals your testimony he steals your victory and the victory of those who would hear it. What has God done for you? Reveal it and God will reward it!

The Shedding of Blood

And almost all things are by the law purged with blood; and without the shedding of blood is no remission. (Hebrews 9:22)

Jesus' blood shed for us satisfied the legal requirement of the law to free us from sin. There had to be a sacrifice for sin to absolve us from sin. Jesus became our sacrifice. And almost all things are purged by blood.

Like the symbolic scarlet thread hanging from Rahab's house (Joshua 2:18) the blood of Jesus protects and delivers us from sin and death. Jesus' ascension to the cross provided a legal restriction and liberating signature for those covered by the blood for salvation. Jesus was crucified to provide the blood that legally delivered us from the penalty of sin, just as the death angel passed over every house in Egypt where the blood appeared. (Exodus 12:13)

When we accepted Jesus as savior of our lives, the blood of Jesus was applied in *our* houses-our bodies, and appears over the doorpost our hearts signifying we are legally covered by Jesus' sacrifice. We are covered in covenant by the blood of Jesus. He became our savior for sin through the shedding of blood and the suffering of the cross.

Life is in the blood and without the shedding of blood there is no remission of sin. Be careful: *If we say we have no sin, we deceive ourselves, and the truth is not in us. (I John 1:8)*

The Lamb of God

And all that dwell upon the earth shall worship him, whose names are not written in the book of life of the Lamb slain from the foundation of the world. (Revelations 13:8)

To legally enter the world, God needed a body. To provide himself a body, He sowed His son in the form of Jesus in the faithful womb of the Virgin Mary.

Jesus had to die to provide the blood for remission of sin. If the rulers of this world had known this, they would not have killed Jesus. They did not see Him as the Lamb of God but a challenge to their religious orders and crucified Him. But if they had not killed Him then there would be no blood to apply and save. *Had they known it they would have not crucified the Lord of glory. (I Corinthians 2:8)*

Recall too that they couldn't take Jesus' life unless He laid it down. (John 10:18)

The word (Jesus) had to submit to death in order to die. The nature of the word is that it lives forever. Therefore, the only way Jesus, the word, could die is to relinquish the eternity of His existence long enough to die and be raised. This also shows us that Jesus could not stay dead because the word cannot be eternally dead. *The word abides forever. (I Peter 1:23)*

God-Spirit
Jesus' spirit
soul
body

Think On These Things

Jesus was a man possessing a divine nature. He was and is as the first Adam was in the beginning. Jesus became the second Adam evidenced by His divine nature. (I Corinthians 15:45) His divine nature is and was the order of man before man fell from God with the exception that His spirit is the very Spirit that is God.

The illustration above demonstrates Jesus in a body, possessing a soul, while His spirit was one with God the Father, who is Spirit. This illustrates His divine nature as well. Note that His Spirit is the same Spirit that is God the Father. They are one and the same Spirit. The divine nature makes Jesus God and renders us godly and able to act divinely.

How do we know that Jesus was both God and man? He was manifested in the flesh (I Timothy 3:16), He wept (John 11:35) and He expressed His will. *Nevertheless not my will, but thine, be done. (Luke 22:42)*

Neither pray I for these alone, but for them also which shall believe on me through their word; that they all may be one; as thou, Father, art in me, and I in thee, that they also may be one in us: that the world may believe that thou hast sent me. (John 17:21, 22)

Reflection 25: A thought about Christmas: In order to have the cross we had to have Christmas. It required blood for our blessing. It required sacrifice for our salvation. There was no pageantry, lights or songs at His crucifixion, only pain and suffering. Remember that Mary, the mother of our Lord, who nursed Jesus, raised Him as a boy and saw the beginning of His ministry, was forced to watch her son die infamously. There was no beauty that we should desire Him.

Unto us a child is born a son is given and the government shall be upon his shoulder. (Isaiah 9:6)

We thank God for Christmas because without Christmas there would be no cross and we would be lost. Each Christmas return to this section and thank God for the Christ of Christmas. Whether you celebrate Christmas or not, celebrate Jesus and that is all that is required.

Friends of God

At once, God is both unfathomable and a familiar friend.

All this talk of salvation and how we are saved sometimes misses the simple truth that, most of all, God desires us as friends. We can be friends of God as the man Moses was a friend of God. (Deuteronomy 34:10)

It may be difficult to believe but the unfathomable indescribable God of all creation longs to be your friend. Yes, God filling the universe longs for your salvation to be the beginning of an eternal fellowship with Him. He is both far and near yet *in him we live and move and have our being. (Acts 17:28) Am I not a God who is near and not far? (Jeremiah 23:23)* No man has seen God at any time and lived but He is seen in all of creation. He is all around you and in you at the same time. He is Christ *in you the hope of glory!* He is God, an unspeakable mystery. He is, was and *is* to come. He is Jesus the expressed image of the invisible God. He is both God and man. He is the God of man yet a friend.

Who can know Him? The voice of God is thunderous in (Job 37:5) yet He speaks in a still small voice. (I Kings 19:12) He is eternal yet shows up in time. He is all powerful but humbled himself and took the form of a baby to save us. He owns the cattle on a thousand hills yet is revealed in the details of our finances. He fills the universe yet saturates our being with His Spirit. In the end, friendship with God is to desire Him. Seek Him until He is found to be a friend.

Now Pray: Today Lord, I approach you as a friend not a foe, as a lover not a lost soul, as a pursuer not a plaintiff, in prayer not as a prisoner. I am saved and not afraid. I am naked and not ashamed.

Reflection 26: In truth, to know God is to be free of the fear of God. Without a doubt you may know God. To love God is to know Him; to know Him is to love Him.

What are your thoughts of God? How do you see Him? Don't be given to cliché' type answers here. Who is God to you? Don't regurgitate who men say He is. Who do you say He is? Only what you think and your relationship to Him matters. Some would quickly answer, "He is my all and all", and don't even know what that means. God cannot be "all and all" to you and possess only a portion of your heart. Some would say, "He's a wheel in the middle of a wheel". What does that mean? Or "He's the center of my Joy". So why don't you have joy? My point is that most people don't know who God is-to them. This is not an area to get super spiritual. You must know God in a real way. To know God is to be known of God, Does He know you?

>God out there
>God in me
>God everywhere
>I can and cannot see.

Father, Son and Holy Spirit

And without controversy great is the mystery of godliness: God was manifest in the flesh, justified in the Spirit, seen of angels, preached unto the Gentiles, believed on in the world, received up into glory.
(I Timothy 3:16)

Who was manifested in the flesh? God as Jesus was manifested in the flesh. Jesus is God. Jesus the Son is Father God in another form. The Holy Ghost is the Spirit of Jesus and God the Father. God the Father, God the Son, and God the Holy Spirit are one not three, they are the same God. They are one and the same-*God is one* not many. God the Father, God the Son, and God the Holy Spirit are three but the same God. God is one God revealed in three forms. You may ask how is it that God can preside on earth by His Spirit and still be on His throne. The answer is: God is His Spirit. *God is a Spirit: and they that worship him must worship him in spirit and in truth. (John 4:24)*

God the Father, God the Son, and God the Holy Spirit are *so* one that they cannot be separated. You cannot divide God and God is revealed in three forms.

Man is like God in his composition. We are spirit, soul, and body but not three persons. We are the same person in different forms. As an example, parents may assume many roles but they remain one person not many. A man may be a husband, father, and minister but remain one person. He is one person represented in different forms.

A further example includes a man and woman in marriage. The man and woman become one by marriage. The woman is the man in another form. Where did she come from? She came out of man. In like manner, God presented Jesus out of himself by his Spirit. By the way, we are God in another form. *Ye are gods, created in his image and likeness.*

To wit, that God was in Christ, reconciling the world unto himself, not imputing their trespasses unto them; and hath committed unto us the word of reconciliation. (2 Corinthians 5:19)

God placed himself in a body and became Jesus. He put himself in Jesus and the word became *flesh and dwelt among us. We beheld his glory, the glory as of the only begotten of the Father, full of grace and truth. (John 1: 14)* In essence, through Jesus God the Father presented himself in another form and you cannot know

God the Father without knowing Jesus. And further, you cannot have fellowship Jesus without fellowship with His Spirit and you cannot have fellowship with God the Father without first accepting Jesus.

Jesus saith unto him, I am the way, the truth, and the life: no man cometh unto the Father, but by me. (John 14:6) Neither is there salvation in any other. (Acts 4:12)

Blaspheming the Holy Ghost

And whosoever shall speak a word against the Son of man, it shall be forgiven him: but unto him that blasphemeth against the Holy Ghost it shall not be forgiven. (Luke 12:10)

The matter of blaspheming the Holy Ghost is a concern and fear of many. This section is not intended to induce more fear but gender a gravity and greater reverence for God.

The only way to become one with God in salvation is by His Spirit. Your union with God is based on your relationship with the Holy Spirit. If you willfully *speak a word against* His Spirit you have no means of connecting or communion with God. The Spirit of God is whom you receive in receiving Jesus to be saved. To reject the Spirit of God is to reject God and lose any means of being in fellowship with God. In this case, God is unable to connect with you by your choice to be separated from Him. There's no way to turn back to God without the Spirit of God. In the end, the offense of blaspheming against the Spirit of God, is unpardonable and will be judged by God.

If we reverse forgive to give-for, we can ask the question: What can God give for one who has rejected His Spirit?

Fear not, because those who have the Spirit of God cannot call Jesus accursed and cannot blaspheme the Spirit of God. *Wherefore I give you to understand, that no man speaking by the Spirit of God calleth Jesus accursed: and that no man can say that Jesus is the Lord, but by the Holy Ghost. (I Corinthians 12:3)* Only reverence God's Spirit and His Spirit will direct you toward God. Do not be afraid that you have blasphemed the Holy Spirit, only reverence Him and you don't need to fear. The fact you have examined yourself on this matter is an indication you are sensitive to the Spirit of God and have not blasphemed the Holy Spirit. Use this light to be more reverent of God and the things of God.

Think On These Things

For Church leaders: Unfortunately, many churches are grieving and quenching the Spirit of God. These are forms of rejecting the Holy Spirit as blaspheming the Holy Spirit is.

The Holy Spirit must be the pastor of your church otherwise your church will have a *show of godliness but deny the power thereof. (2 Timothy 3:5)* In following, a church where the Holy Spirit is not pastor will eventually succumb to a pattern of quenching the Spirit and grieving Him by omitting Him from His role of leadership and guidance in the church. *He (the Spirit) will guide you into all truth. (John 16:13)* Where the Spirit of God is leading, we must follow. Our programs must cease when His presence is prevailing. The church that is not Spirit-led is not Spirit-fed. In (I Corinthians 2:4), Paul says,

And my speech and my preaching was not with enticing words of man's wisdom, but in demonstration of the Spirit and of power.

Once the Holy Spirit is ministering, who needs a minister? If worship overflows into the announcements and preaching time, this means the Holy Spirit is operating and teaching and every other agenda must be silenced. **It grieves God that the things of God have become more important than God in His church.** When the Spirit descends His descent may appear disorderly but in reality He becomes the order and we must then relent to His will. If not, the church will be fervent but not on fire. Consider that *He will burn up the chaff with unquenchable fire. (Matthew 3:11, 12)*

How many Sunday services have been prematurely ended because the clock said it was time? How many have said NO to the move of God because it was time for church presentations. Have we declined God's presence for our presentations?

Now Pray: Welcome Holy Spirit in every area of my life and ministry. Take control of my tongue and give me utterance that I might speak your will and receive revelation for living. Forgive the church for her denial of your leadership and move upon us again in great power, anointing and glory.

Ask For Bread

If a son shall ask bread of any of you that is a father, will he give him a stone? Or if he ask a fish, will he for a fish give him a serpent? Or if he shall ask an egg, will he offer him a scorpion? If ye then, being evil know how to give good gifts unto your children; how much more shall your heavenly Father give the Holy Spirit to them that ask him? (Luke 11:11-13)

Notice in this passage that the key to receiving is asking. Asking is power in the Kingdom of God and with God. Only by asking may you receive anything from God. Why? Asking, positions us by humility to receive from God. *Humble yourselves therefore under the mighty hand of God, that he may exalt you in due time. (1 Peter 5:6)*

He said unto them, Have you received the Holy Ghost since ye believed? And they said unto him, we have not so much as heard whether there be any Holy Ghost. (Acts 19:2)

This passage indicates a subsequent encounter with the Spirit of God following salvation which is the baptism, immersion and induction of believers into the Holy Spirit. This is the same enduing descent of the Spirit of God that the disciples experienced on the day of Pentecost. Yes, you may be saved but not filled with the Holy Spirit. You have the Spirit of God in you to secure and consummate salvation but that is different from having your entire being saturated in the Spirit of God by His filling. To *be filled* with the Spirit of God is to come under the influence or dictates of the Spirit like a drunkard under the influence of alcohol. The drunkard's walk and talk are changed. Your walk and talk will change too as the Spirit guides you. We can verify this as true based on the account of the day of Pentecost in (Acts 2:13-15)

Others mocking said, These men are full of new wine. But Peter, standing up with the eleven, lifted up their voice, and said unto them, Ye men of Judea, and all ye that dwell in Jerusalem, be this known unto you, and hearken to my words: For these are not drunken, as ye suppose, Seeing it is but the third hour of the day.

Notice this passage begins by mentioning *Peter standing.* Remember Peter running, denying, and cursing away his relationship with Jesus? When you are filled or empowered by the Spirit of God, you begin to stand where you formerly ran. You begin to speak boldly as the Spirit gives you utterance. You become an effective witness of Jesus Christ.

Without the Holy Spirit leading your life you may be on your way to heaven but possess little power to live like God, witness effectively, or operate in the gifts of God to His glory.

Be not drunk with wine; be ye filled with the Spirit. (Ephesians 5:18) To be filled with the Spirit of God is a call and petition extended to the believer. You may choose not to be filled, but your spiritual walk will suffer. Notice this is a choice and you only need to ask to receive. The reason Jesus told His disciples to wait in Jerusalem for the promised Holy Spirit, is because they needed the leadership of the Spirit and the power of His person to accomplish kingdom business and so do you.

Reflection 27: Where are the miracles and demonstration of power today that were experienced in the book of Acts? Could it be that we have neglected the Holy Spirit as the worker of miracles? The Holy Spirit was and is the worker of miracles but we must allow Him to direct our times of worship and ministry to see miracles manifested. If the Holy Spirit wrecks a perfectly prepared program, remember He is the Pastor.

If you doubt we need to be filled with the Holy Spirit with the evidence of speaking in other tongues, then read about the disciples' weak attempts at ministry before Pentecost. Then notice their exploits in the book of Acts on the day of Pentecost and following. *Then Peter, filled with the Holy Ghost, said unto them, Ye rulers of the people, and elders of Israel, If we this day be examined of the good deed done to the impotent man, by what means he is made whole; Be it known unto you all, and to all the people of Israel, that by the name of Jesus Christ of Nazareth, whom ye crucified, whom God raised from the dead, even by him doth this man stand here before you whole. (Acts 4:8-10)*

The same Peter who denied Jesus three times now boldly proclaimed His name and began doing the works that Jesus did. His example proves we cannot be as Jesus is and do as He does without His Spirit. And we must wait on Him as the disciples did on the day of Pentecost. How do we receive the Holy Spirit? We receive generously from God by simply asking.

Come Holy Spirit
Like a dove
Breathe on us again
With power from above

God is willing to do in you and through you what you cannot do in your own power. Your spiritual life will be filled with frustrations in following Christ without the filling of His Spirit.

What was the difference between receiving the Spirit the way the disciples received, in (John 20:22) and the enduing Spiritual deluge on the day of Pentecost? The disciples' experience before Jesus' glorious ascension back to heaven allowed them to conceive salvation by the Spirit of God. *Note: You must first receive the Spirit in salvation to receive the second enduing of power with the evidence of speaking other tongues.* The Day of Pentecost was an outpouring of the promised Holy Spirit that empowered the disciples- now apostles, to become witnesses of Jesus in every place by demonstration and power.

In Jesus' Name

What's in the name of Jesus? No other name causes as much division and contention as the name of Jesus. You may say God in many settings and this is widely accepted. You can say Father as well and there will be little reaction. But when any professes Jesus Christ and speaks His name, there is a visceral response in every place. No one can be neutral about Jesus. Either you love Him or deny Him. The entire world has to make a decision on Jesus. Why is this? There is no other name given under heaven whereby we must be saved. There is power in the name of Jesus! At *the name of Jesus every knee shall bow and every tongue confesses that Jesus is Lord. (Philippians 2:10)*

God has sanctioned all He is through Jesus. Access to God is by Jesus. No man can come to the Father, but by Him. His name is who Jesus is, and God endorses only that name. The name of Jesus is the name of God. All the names of God throughout the bible are given in one name-Jesus. Therefore, Jehovah-Rapha, God your healer of all diseases, Jehovah-Jireh, The Lord will provide, Jehovah-Nissi, The Lord is my banner, are all the names of Jesus because Jesus is God.

> *His eyes were as a flame of fire, and on his head were many crowns; and he had a name written, that no man knew, but he himself. And he was clothed with vesture dipped in blood: and his name is called The Word of God. (Revelation 19:12, 13)*

Jesus' name represents the authority of God. You may come in another name but only the authority of Jesus' name moves both heaven and earth. *In the name of Jesus Christ of Nazareth rise up and walk. (Acts 3:6)* In the name of Jesus there is authorization for healing, deliverance, casting out devils, subduing sickness and securing salvation. *He hath given him a name* which is authority and power. And His name releases the fullness of God and the glory of His person to meet every temporal and eternal need. Devils tremble at the name of Jesus and when Jesus said *I give you power over all the power of the enemy,* that power was in His name. Your prayers are all fulfilled and honored in the name of Jesus and that explains why we pray in the name of Jesus. If we pray in any other name, access is denied to God.

Think On These Things

Now Pray: Father God may every man hear the sweet name of Jesus and taste and see that God is good. Amen.

Reflection 28: God has put all things under Jesus' feet. (Ephesians 1:22) Therefore, when you come to God you must come through Jesus. If you speak in power you must speak in the name of Jesus. When you pray in the name of Jesus you are confessing all things are submitted and settled based on who He is. To pray for your family in Jesus' name is to submit them to His authority and power and experience their deliverance. We win all battles and subdue all enemies in the name of Jesus!

> Nothing more can I proclaim
> But all that is in Jesus' name.

Go tell it!

Jesus offered salvation to the Woman at the well in the fourth chapter of the gospel of John and eventually she became a witness of Him. On this occasion, the never ending, ever giving God interjected himself into a temporary situation. **Don't allow a temporary situation to become a fixed destination in your life.** Jesus asked her to give Him a drink. Why would He ask someone who had nothing to give, to give him something? Jesus knew that the real woman inside the woman held eternal value. In the end, she *did* have something to give; she had herself to give. But hadn't she already given to the count of five husbands and the man she was with was not her husband? The difference was that giving to Jesus caused her to tap into an eternal supply by union with his eternal being. Jesus' request was her invitation to indulge deeply into the aquifers of salvation.

To satisfy Jesus is to be satisfied. Jesus basically said to her, "satisfy me and you will be eternally satisfied." He was saying to her, "give me your best and I'll give you my best and a release into rest." He was saying, "Invest in me and you will reap eternal rewards." Jesus was inviting a woman who had only been promised and engaged to enter into true intimacy. He was asking the woman to do something she had done before without success.

Isn't it true of us too that we often miss God because of relationship disappointments and lost love? We often decline invitations to communion with Jesus due to thirsty unfulfilled hearts.

To conceal her pain, the woman at the well became religiously avoidant while talking about worship. She became lawful not liberated. She spoke like a Christian but was only casting a web for her weaknesses. How often do you change the subject to avoid your pain? This isn't a cure or release into God's rest. In fact, by doing so, you are avoiding God's best.

Eventually, Jesus led this woman to true worship. Becoming one with Him in worship caused her life to overflow eternally. In the past giving to others bankrupted her, by giving to Jesus she became eternally wealthy. **God knows our stories and has glory for each story!**

Jesus touched her in a way she had never been touched, without touching her. He made a deposit in her by requiring a withdrawal from her. He drew out of her deep place by bringing her to a place of giving. And as she gave she began to overflow, eternally.

Think On These Things

We also know that Jesus took a risk to engage the woman at the well.

The Jews and Samaritans have no dealings. (John 4:9)

Like Jesus, you too must place yourself at risk to help someone get to Jesus. You must leave your comfort zone, risk your reputation, or risk offending a crowd, to lead others to your savior. This may require that you introduce truth into the lives of others. Then they will be positioned to be saved.

Do you know that the woman at the well was really seeking someone honorable to give her honor to? She was looking for someone whose weight of glory would cause her to rise.

Someone is waiting on you to place a demand on their eternal significance. They're waiting for your witness to endorse them as witnesses of Jesus. The world is waiting on you to tell the story that gives God glory. *How that while we were yet sinners he died for the ungodly and sinner. (Romans 5:8)*

Some Christians forget they were once sinners and fail to witness. As this woman, go and tell what Jesus has done for you. (John 4:29)

That which you have both seen and heard and seen in me, do (Philippians 4:9). Do you know that you are deep and full? Go and give until you are eternally filled. Perhaps, as the church of Jesus Christ we are too busy preaching to one another to *go into all world.*

Now Pray: Lord fill me to full that I might overflow as a witness into all the world. Amen

Reflection 29: Is it true that once we are saved, we are always saved? Is our salvation eternally secured?

No one will presume to know who is going to heaven or hell. The word of God says God is married to the backslider. (Jeremiah 3:14) The bible speaks of the *very elect being deceived*, and *a great falling away* in the last days.

Since grace abounds shall we continue in sin? (Romans 6:1) Grace is not granted that we may *continue in sin.* Jesus said, *Many will say to me in that day, Lord, Lord, have we not prophesied in thy name? and in thy name have cast out devils? And in thy name done many wonderful works? And then will I profess unto them, I never knew you: depart from me, ye that work iniquity.* (Matthew 7:22, 23)

For the saved and ministers of God, we cannot presume to be citizens of heaven because at one time we professed Christ and did certain works for God in His name. We must *work out our salvation with fear and trembling* without disbanding grace.

Not every one that saith unto me Lord, Lord, shall enter into the kingdom of heaven; but he that doeth the will of my Father which is in heaven. (Matthew 7:22)

The notion of being saved and always being saved is subject to every man's will. If by will and choice we may choose Jesus, then by will and choice we may deny Him as Peter did. Adam and Eve were eternally secured in the presence of God. However, by choice and will they chose outside the will of God and were lost. The point is that we must *follow on to know the Lord* and receive His *grace in time of need while seeing the end of our faith, the salvation of our souls.* We cannot presume eternal salvation if we willfully leave the security of His salvation. *Except these abide in the ship, ye cannot be saved.* (Acts 27:31)

If you die saved or God's Spirit dwells in you upon His descent for the saints (saved ones), you will be with God for eternity-that is heaven. If you die unsaved or God's Spirit does not dwell in you upon His return, you will not ascend but descend for eternity separated from God-that is hell.

Therefore we ought to give the more earnest heed to the things which we have heard, lest at any time we should let them slip. For if the word spoken by angels was steadfast, and every transgression and disobedience received a just reward; How shall we escape, if we neglect so great salvation; which at the first began to be spoken by the Lord, and was confirmed unto us by them that heard him...(Hebrews 2:1-3)

And Further

For it is impossible for those who were once enlightened, and have tasted of the heavenly gift, and were made partakers of the Holy Ghost, and have tasted the good word of God, and the powers of the world to come, if they shall fall away, to renew them again unto repentance; seeing they crucify to themselves the Son of God afresh, and put him to an open shame. (Hebrews 6:4-6)

And finally

But he that shall endure unto the end, the same shall be saved. (Matthew 24:13)

Many believe we will go to hell for what we have done. We certainly must give an account of our stewardship. But many will go to hell for what they have not done as well. Your stewardship is accounted for. What are you doing with what you have been given?

Chapter Notes

_____

_____

_____

_____

That was the true light, which lighteth every man that cometh into the world. (John 1:9)

FAITH PAGES

Now faith is...

Chapter 3

Now faith is...

Now faith is the substance of things hoped for, the evidence of things not seen. (Hebrews 11:1)

And Caleb stilled the people before Moses, and said, Let us go up at once, and possess it; for we are well able to overcome it. (Numbers 13:30)

Fear is intimidated and says, "There are giants in the land!" While faith retorts, "We are the giants in the land!" You ARE the giants in the land!

What did Caleb and Joshua see that the other spies did not when marching toward to the Promised Land? Caleb and Joshua looked with eyes of faith and had a different report. The other spies looked with eyes of fear and became grasshoppers in their OWN eyes. Fear or faith determines how you see life. Your eyes can and do affect your faith. Like your external senses you have internal organs for sight and hearing. You may develop your spiritual eyes and ears to see by faith. This is important because what you see and how you see can infect your faith and determine whether you succeed in life.

Now faith comes by hearing and hearing by the

word of God. Fear comes by hearing too. What are you hearing-faith or fear? Disease may say you will die, what do you hear? What are you hearing? Are you hearing faith or fear? If our hearts may be affected by fear and faith, how important is hearing and seeing? They are important because what enters your hidden eyes and ears soon enters your heart.

Are you aware that giants of fear and mountains of intimidation speak? Giants and mountains are made by fear and conquered by faith. In faith, David said he would take Goliath's head. *I will smite thee, and take thine head from thee. (I Kings 17:46)* David ran into the fight. Are you running into the fight or back to safety?

Like David, prepare yourself to intimidate, intimidation, to overcome overwhelming, to subdue your fears by faith. If we succumb to fear we become timid toy soldiers not soldiers in the army of the Lord.

By the way, is it okay to be intimidated? Should Christians have fear? Isn't fear natural?

You were created with a measure of faith not fear. Fear is learned not natural otherwise God would have given you a measure of fear rather than a measure of faith to live by. You may naturally feel fear but fear is not natural.

The only way to overcome fear is by faith. Feed your faith not your fears and you will *be* the giant in the land.

Because there are times we experience fear, pray like David in (Psalm 56:3, 4)

What time I am afraid, I will trust in thee. In God I will praise his word, in God I have put my trust; I will not fear what flesh can do unto me.

Think On These Things

Now Pray: Lord may the blood of Jesus be applied to my ear gate and eye gate that I might not entertain any perverse thing. Protect these entrances to my soul and thereby protect my heart and the future residing within me.

Reflection 30: Fear intimidates and separates. *Whatsoever is not of faith is sin. (Romans 14:23)* Whatever is sin separates.

Faith is a spirit, so is fear. The spirit of faith gives you the ability to create and dominate your world. Fear gives you the unenviable ability to fail and be dominated by every situation and circumstance. *For God hath not given us the spirit of fear; but of power, and of love, and of a sound mind. (2 Timothy 1:7)*

Satan is that spirit of fear. Now, think of a spirit as giving one the ability to be and do. For example, the spirit of faith gives one the ability to express unusual faith. The spirit of prophesy gives one the ability to prophesy on occasion. The spirit of fear gives one the ability to fail while the spirit of faith gives one the ability to succeed. Not only does faith give one the ability to succeed but gains access and authority to godly success. Faith is, as you have heard, the believer's authority. And we have *the* measure of faith to combat *the* spirit of fear.

Father of faith	Godly realm-Unseen of God
Faith	Eternal realm-Unseen but real
Fear	Temporal realm-seen

The illustration of faith shows us that faith is of a higher order than fear. However, if you live in fear you then become subject to the things on the mundane temporal level. An example is Peter walking on water. Peter was in the earthy temporal realm but at the word of God which is from the eternal realm -like faith, he was able to overcome natural gravity to rise above a turbulent sea. However, when he began to fear he sank below the level of faith and succumbed to the waves of doubt and unbelief on the lower plane of fear. Peter's example also shows how quickly we may revert to fear soon after walking on water.

What you focus on you will soon be overcome by or graduate to.

Faith is the higher plane we are called to live on. By which the scriptures says we may *quench all the fiery darts of the enemy. (Ephesians 6:16)* But if you live in fear you will be dominated by the temporal earthly realm. This is the realm we see with our physical eyes and call natural. If you live by faith, which supersedes and has authority over the natural temporal realm, you will dominate in life as God intended. You will live on earth as Jesus did. *As he is so are we in the world. (1 John 4:17)*

Think On These Things

Now Pray: Lord I thank you by faith the things that would subdue me are subdued by me. May I hold fast my profession of faith without wavering.

Reflection 31: You can do in faith what you can never do in fear. How you see will determine what you see. If you look at life with the eyes of fear you will sink below God's purpose for your life. If you look at life with eyes of faith you will see limitless possibilities!

Faith Has Taught Us Faith!

In (I Samuel 17:36) David said, Thy servant slew both the lion and the bear: and this uncircumcised Philistine shall be as one of them, seeing he hath defiled the armies of the living God.

David knew that he had the legal right and authority over Goliath and the Philistine was already defeated by his position against God's people. *But if it be of God, ye cannot overthrow it; lest haply ye be found even to fight against God. (Acts 5:39)* You must know that your position of faith obligates God to defend you. Like David, you also develop an anointing for battle as you fight each fight of faith.

If God be for us, who can be against us? (Romans 8:31) David was anointed for battle, he knew who he was, he was called and commissioned of God, his faith had been on trial and faith had taught him faith. Faith has taught you faith! In other words, what you have endured through is working for you now and in each future battle.

Therefore, *Count it all Joy when you fall in divers trial and temptations, the trial of your faith being more precious than that of Gold. (James 1:2)*

Put on the whole armor of God... not the armor of tradition, conformity, or fear.

Above all put on the shield of faith, wherewith ye shall be able to quench all the fiery darts of the wicked. (Ephesians 6:16)

How is David's ordeal of faith any different than your own? Have you not faced your most formidable opponents? Have you not tested them as you have been tested and found that you too can conquer your lion, your bear and the giant to come? Do you know that David killed Goliath before he engaged the battle? Do you know Goliath was without a covenant with God therefore his head was not covered in battle? Do you know that you will always win because *the battle is not yours, but God's. (2 Chronicles 20:15)*

Think on these things

You may be in the biggest test of your life today, facing the most imposing figure of your imagination, but the answer is still the same. You are well able! In the end, how you see a giant will determine whether you will conquer a giant. Are your inner eyes full of faith or fear?

Now Pray: Lord I pray that my faith does not fail. Help me to stand, pursue, create, and elevate to possess all that you promised, in Jesus' name, amen.

Reflection 32: The giant you're facing today may be formidable but just as defeat able as Goliath was to David. *Then said David to the Philistine, Thou comest to me with a sword and spear and javelin, but I come to you in the name of the Lord of Host…(I Samuel 17:45).* They have a sword, you have the Lord!

Is There Anything Too Hard, with God?

But Jesus beheld them, and said unto them, With men this is impossible; but with God all things are possible. (Matthew 19:26)

Is it a surprise to you that God is the God of the impossible? The key to this verse is, "with God". God is extreme and excessive and whatever God is in becomes like God. God is limitless and boundless, extreme eternal and overflowing. With Him, impossible becomes possible, not enough becomes more than enough because *He is able to do exceeding abundantly above all we ask or think according to his power that is at work in us. (Ephesians 3:20).* Your limits are not God's limits. His limitless existence is your limitless possibilities.

Sarah laughed when God said she and Abraham would have a son in their old age. (Genesis 18:12) It seemed impossible but the word proceeded from an "all things possible" God. Abraham had been tested before when God said he would be the father of a multitude. What he could not fathom faith was waiting to reveal.

Examine the evidence of faith not the evidence of present circumstances. Look again at your situation with the eyes of faith. Go on and see the unseen and hear the unheard, then declare: *With God all things are possible!* All you need is a word from God.

What has God said? His word will not return to Him void without accomplishing what He sent it to change. By faith, you will experience changes in your life and begin to live in an unlimited way. This will happen when you believe that God is the God of impossible things. Is there anything too hard for God?

Isn't it time you get out of the boat of fearful impossibilities and take up water walking? Like Peter, ask God to call you to the impossible, "bid me come" and He will respond, COME!

You will find that when your in God's will, He is a "no limits" God!

The word of God will sustain you in every circumstance. His word is a proceeding word. This means what God spoke is still speaking. What He spoke is speaking and will yet speak. It is therefore paramount that you apply His word in every circumstance. The word is proceeding. If you live by the voice of His word you will prevail; if you live by the voice of your storm or your own fear, you will sink beneath the surface of circumstances and drown.

Peter did what Jesus did by walking on the water until he meditated on conditions. Circumstances hold a gravity and weight that will sink you if you live by them. *The Just shall live by faith! (Habakkuk 2:4)*

The world is decidedly a place of disorder. The word of God is God's order. Now imagine there is a hurricane in the area of your life. But you are safely on the plane of faith above the level of the hurricane. Similarly, there are no worries in life for those who overcome the elements of life by faith-worries are beneath them. They are not affected because they are living at the level of faith not fear.

Fear will subject you to storms and *fear hath torment. (I John 4:18)* Faith will cause you to elevate rather than capitulate. Whatever it is today, say: "I'm living above this at the level of faith." "I'm not admiring my storms, I'm not conditioned by my conditions, and I'm not living by circumstantial evidence because faith *is* my evidence." In light of this, whatever has you down should not hold power to keep you down.

Think On These Things

Do you know that God sees storms differently? He sees them from a level that would allow him to speak to storms and say to you, "Fear not". Is it possible that you're an overcomer and not aware of it? *Nay in all these things, we are more than conquerors through him that loved us. (Romans 8:37)*

Storms are not permanent; they are temporarily *"working together for good to them that love the lord and are called according to his purpose." (Romans 8:28)* Speak to your storms; *Peace be still* and they will obey you from the plane of faith and you will live to testify.

That the trial of your faith, being more precious than of gold that perisheth, though it be tried in the fire, might be found unto praise and glory at the appearing of Jesus Christ. (1 Peter 1:7)

Now Pray: Lord summons me to the arena of the impossible, to see the invisible, appropriate the intangible, and make known the unknown as though it already existed.

Reflection 33: Don't live down to circumstances, live up to the word of God. Blot out your doubt and fortify your most holy faith.

Overcoming Gravity

For our light affliction, which is but for a moment

worketh for us a far more exceeding and eternal weight of glory. (2 Corinthians. 4:17)

Undoubtedly, there is gravity to life. It tends to push us downward and keep us from advancing onward. However, the weight of God's word is weightier than the weight of the world causing us to ascend above the things that tend to keep us down and bound. Jesus was the word made flesh and even the grave couldn't keep Him down. *O Grave where is your victory; Oh death where is your sting! He that descended is also he that ascended led captivity captive and gave gifts unto men. (Ephesians 4:10)*

The world is too heavy for you. It is too complicated and tension filled. Today you need the weight of God's word to bear the weight of the world. Say with me: I can do all things through Christ who strengthens me. It's not you; it is Christ in you, the hope of glory. Are you the Lord of your life? If so, you're feeling the weight of the world.

Hear God say: *Come unto me all ye that labor and are heavy laden, and I will give you rest. Take my yoke upon you, and learn of me; for I am meek and lowly in heart: and ye shall find rest unto your souls. For my yoke is easy, and my burden is light. (Matthew 11:30)*

We have the yoke of abiding and the burden of believing. No one is denying the trouble in this world but *Take no thought for tomorrow* because your Father in heaven knows what you have need of. *But seek first the kingdom of God, and his righteousness; and all these things will be added unto you. (Matthew 6:33)* God invites us to believe Him, to seek the kingdom and He will provide all our needs *according to his riches in glory by Christ Jesus. (Philippians 4:19)*

If a millionaire told you not to worry because he would meet all your needs, it is almost certain you would instantly be relieved at his word. God has riches in glory unlimited, why do you then carry the weight and responsibility of living?

The word of God will always rise above the world. The weight of the word is weightier (more glorious) than the weight (burden) of the world.

Expectations: God Size Them!

Then he which had received the one talent came and said, Lord, I knew thee that thou are an hard man, reaping where thou hast not sown, and gathering where thou hast not strawed: And I was afraid, and went and hid thy talent in the earth: lo, there thou hast that is thine. (Matthew 25:24, 25)

This servant's fear eliminated any expectations he might have had and reduced God's investment to a loss.

How many are prepared to bring an accusation against God for their lack of progress or success in life and ministry? How many have quit on God's deepest purpose and walk unfilled in the earth? It's not God's fault.

Being confident in this very thing, that he which hath begun a good work in you will perform it until the day of Jesus Christ… (Philippians 1:6)

Expectation is an often undetectable element of faith and as such it is overlooked. God's question to you today is: Do you want to live in fear and offer excuses, or do you want to increase what God has invested in you?

We tend to think we are submitting huge petitions to God but we rarely do. Many of the things we are asking God to do, we can do by our own faith. Try giving God something "God-size" to perform in your life and know that God will always give you a formidable giant to confront you. He will allow something insurmountable to embattle you. He knows that it is bigger than you but not bigger than Him. He allows this so He might be glorified in you and that you might learn to trust Him. Is it too big for you? Then it must be God-size!

You must expect more, higher, and deeper of God because God will always perform at the level of your expectations. Expectation is an overlooked element of faith that moves your faith in the direction of possessing the promises of God. If you never consider a thing possible, how can you ever believe for it? If you never turn in the direction of your promised land, how can you ever take steps toward it? God will reciprocate your faith but you must raise your expectations. If you expect spiritual tents when God has mansions for you; He will not give you greater than your expectation. You are bound to live in a tent.

Abraham had difficulty expecting one son when in faith God had generations of sons in his loins. If you expect little you get little; expect much and you will receive more than enough. And remember just because something has never been done does not mean it will go undone. And don't assume because you have a need that God will automatically fill it. *Ask and the door will be opened. Seek and you will find. (Matthew 7:7)*

Remember the blind man in (Mark 10: 51)? Jesus asked him what he wanted. This man was blind and Jesus asked him what his expectation was. Initially, the man offers excuses regarding his condition. He basically said, "What had happened was" and offered excuses. This approach placed no demand on Jesus to bless him. However, when he changed his position by changing his expectation, he received his sight. His expectation placed a demand by faith on Jesus to heal him. If you never consider or expect God to do greater things, how can he perform them? *Without faith it is impossible to please God. (Hebrews 11:6)*

Expect more than you ever have before! Most people expect something small; why not expect that and more?

The Good Fight

I have fought a good fight, I have finished my course, I have kept the faith… (2 Timothy. 4:7)

Paul resounds that he has fought a good fight. The good fight is the fight God has called you to, not people. Leadership is challenged with the temptation to compromise. **You must be willing to die for what you believe in or watch what you believe in trampled.**

Saul compromised and lost his high calling. The people of God wanted a god they could see so Aaron allowed them to craft a golden calf. Eli allowed his sons to live ungodly and lost his prophetic office. Men and women of God, you must know who you are and what you are called to. You must know what God has said and what God has not said to engage in the battle for souls victoriously.

Wherefore the rather, brethren, give diligence to make your calling and election sure: for if ye do these things, ye shall never fail.
(2 Peter 1:10)

If God says kill all the enemies' people and the animals with them; then you must obey Him and not the voice of the people.

And he who will save his life will lose it and he who will lose his life will save it. (Luke 9:24)

Remembering Jesus, *who for the Joy that was set before him endured the cross despising the shame. (Hebrews 12:2)*

As a leader, you will be tested and there will be invitations to walk in error. The primary way to guard your heart against this is by obedience to God's word. You may also seek those who will hold you accountable.

Let a righteous man smite me; it shall be a kindness: and let him reprove me; it shall be an excellent oil, which shall not break my head. (Psalm 141:5)

Think On These Things

It is the rare leader who stands on his values, selflessly serves others, shuns compromise and corruption and is willing to die on purpose, that does not achieve some measure of greatness.-Rogers J Greene Jr.

Now Pray: Lord, help me to finish the race you have given me. Lord, grant me the grace to lead the people of God into our promised land without a detour or disaster, in Jesus name, amen!

Reflection 34: It's to the glory of God that you finish what God started in you. Fight the fight you were called to fight, obey the voice of God and finish your race. Having done all to stand, finish!

Living without a Doubt

Be careful for nothing; but in every thing by prayer and supplication with thanksgiving let your requests be made known unto God
(Philippians 4:6)

You can't both live life and worry about it. Either you will live life and not worry or worry and not live.
Sometimes the brook dries up or God changes His methods and provides manna from heaven. In some instances, we then lose our confidence. Indeed He will change how He meets your need. He knows you have need of things before you ask Him. He knows you need job changes, living changes, and family adjustments. But to be completely sustained you must be totally dependent. You must trust or go bust. You must be totally dependent upon God as your source. You must trust, abide, stay, and remain in Him. *Abide in me and in you. (John 15:3)* Too many people are trying to make a living rather than stay in position. Be careful that your

worries over life don't separate you from your source. Worry demonstrates a lack of trust in God. Indeed, to doubt God is to be separated from godly provisions. *Take no thought for your life. (Luke 12:22)*

It is true that sometimes we doubt God because the new terrain of faith is unfamiliar. He may be providing manna and leading you into your promised land but you may prefer Egypt's bondage because you are most familiar with that system. But *My God shall supply all your need according to his riches in glory by Christ Jesus. (Philippians 4:19)*

And

I have been young, and now am old; yet have I not seen the righteous forsaken, nor his seed begging bread. (Psalm 37:25)

Who are the righteous? They are those who by faith in God have been *made righteous.* They have been established by faith in right standing with God and therefore are positioned to prosper. They are justified to be satisfied. An indication you are not righteous is the anxiety you sense and the peace you have forfeited.

By now you know that worry does not work. In fact, worry works against you and the will of God for your life. Be assured, *he will never leave you nor forsake you.*

Your bills are not bigger than God's purpose. God's intention is to feed you even in a famine. *In famine he shall redeem thee from death: and in war from the power of the sword. (Job 5:20)*

Think On These Things

God will come to you today with provision because He is God and you are His own. He only requires your trust and obedience. Fear not, He is able *to do exceeding; abundantly above all you can ask or think.* Think of that: God is meeting needs you cannot think to ask him to fill.

If He fed five thousand He will certainly feed you in every area of your life. He provided manna in the wilderness; He will feed you and your children. Now go on and believe God! Believe God and not the circumstances!

Now Pray: God is my source and supply. As he fed Elijah by the brook through a raven; he will more than meet my needs in life and ministry.

Reflection 35: Many are talking about difficult economic times. The truth is there have always been difficult economic times. However, God has not changed and still generates streams in the desert and water in the wilderness. *He clave the rocks in the wilderness, and gave them drink as out of the great depths. He brought streams also out of the rock, and caused waters to run down like rivers. (Psalm 78:15, 16)* Are you in a dry place in your life? Trust God and live without a doubt!

Teach Your Tongue

But the tongue can no man tame; it is an unruly evil, full of deadly poison. (James 3:8)

What you sow will grow and bare fruit in your life. Your words are seed sown. Your words represent your future in seed form. You must say what God says to see what God has spoken.

If your doctor says you have 6 months to live, you cannot confess that. To do so would be to confirm disease, become one with disease and likely die. On the other hand, if you confess with your mouth and believe in your heart that by His stripes you *were* healed, you confirm and sanction healing provided by Jesus' death on the cross. You are healed!

Speak the world only! What are you saying? What are you dictating by your speaking? Every word you speak or articulate with your mouth out of your heart is heard and judged. Every thought has a voice. God accounts for words spoken and unspoken yet heard. He hears both. **Watch your mouth you must eat those words.** *Death and life are in the power of the tongue: and they that love it shall eat the fruit therefore of.* (Proverbs 18:21)

Conclusively, the most powerful mechanism of faith you possess is your tongue. The enemy of your soul can't create but you can. He will use circumstances to provoke you to say what he wants to sow in your life. He knows what you say you will receive. Therefore, he will attack your mind with the voice of thoughts to influence your speaking. In other words, he will attempt to move you to say what he wants to sow in your life.

By the way, the enemy wants you to be so rational that you reason faith to be irrational. He wants you to forfeit the fortunes of faith for a lack of physical evidence. Of course, faith is not rational but it is substantive. Whatever it is, faith for it; is evidence of it!

Given these realities, we all have the test of our tongue. Our tongue is our test. Every tongue has a test. What you say you will eventually see manifested in your life. Take the time to teach your tongue the words of God and never speak in fear, anger, or frustration.

The tongue of the wise useth knowledge aright: but the mouth of fools poureth out foolishness. (Proverbs 15:2)

Think On These Things

Why do we tend to exaggerate our pain and own things undesirable? For example, "My head is killing me!" to describe a headache. Is it really? Or we say things like, "My Diabetes", "My heart condition", "My high blood pressure". Sticks and stones may break your bones but words can kill you!

Now Pray: Set a guard over my mouth, O Lord; keep watch over the door of my lips. (Psalm 141:3)

Reflection 36: How many of you are aware that we frequently say things orally and internally unaware of what we're saying. Please beware that if you say it in your heart; you still said it. And if you say it in your heart it will eventually proceed out of your mouth. *If thou shalt say in thine heart, These nations are more than I; how can I dispossess them? (Deuteronomy 7:17)*

The Measure of Faith

God created man in His spiritual image in the image of God created He them. God breathed the immaterial man into the material man and man became a living soul. And because man is a spirit like God, we breathe things into existence too. Man is a creator like God is *the* creator so man can say like God said, "Let there be…" and it will be. *That whosoever shall say unto this mountain, Be thou removed, and be thou cast into the sea; and shall not doubt in his heart, but shall believe that those things which he saith shall come to pass; he shall have whatsoever he saith. (Mark 11:23)*

Every man saved or not, Christian or not, has *the* measure of faith. Our God-given measure of faith is the ability to create or call those things that are not as thou they already existed. You were created to create whatever you say. "To say" is not only to say but intelligently design, articulate, form, fix, and fashion what you will. Why don't you open your mouth and design your life?

And out of the ground the Lord God formed every beast of the field, and every fowl of the air; and brought them unto Adam to see what he would call them: and whatsoever Adam called every living creature, that was the name thereof. (Genesis 2:19)

Adam created in the image of God was given naming rights. He had *the* measure of faith to create. He had never seen a fish or a bird but he had the ability to call them what he willed. You have naming rights! You can call whatever exist whatsoever you desire. And you can call into existence whatever you want to see. *They are created now, and not from the beginning. (Isaiah 48:7)* You can create and recreate your world. God has given you the authority of faith to create. If something is not working in your life, call it what you want and it will become what you say-by faith.

Think On These Things

How do we apply this measure of faith in our lives? Like God, when you speak your words go out with your spirit to create what you say. Therefore, whether saved or not you have the ability to create. However, when your born again spirit speaks under the authority of God's Spirit and God's words, then you create according to the will of God.

In the beginning "God said" and His Spirit hovered or percolated over chaos and His word was performed. He said, "Let there be light" and there was light! Your spirit goes out with your words as God's word goes out with his Spirit to bring into existence the things unseen. If you don't see it; say it until you see it. If God said so, then you say so, until His Spirit performs it. Speak over the chaos of your life the order of God's words and where there is a void and no form there will be light and a new life.

Now Pray: Lord, I choose life, I choose wholeness and health and healing in my mind body and spirit; According to your word I am blessed in the city and in the field. I am now blessed when I come and go. See Deuteronomy 28:1-14 and confess all that God has for you in the present and future tense. Now believe you receive when you pray then you will have whatsoever you say when you say it; not when you see it.

Let's create: Take a mirror or a pair of eyeglasses and create a frost by blowing on them. You have just created! Or blow into the cold outside and you will see what you have breathed. So it is when you speak by faith. In both examples, you have "God-breathed" something into existence and so it is spiritually speaking.

As it relates to creativity, relationships often die for a lack of creativity. How is that two people created to create, fall victim to living together in a routine unadventurous way? Your relationships require effort; the effort of creating. It requires great quantities of imagination and revelation to create a great relationship. Draw on your God-given creative ability to create a marriage, a business, or church that is bounding with newness of life. When you stop creating in any area of your life, whether that is marriage, ministry, or business, that area is hopelessly given to tarnish and ruin. Want a better life? Create it! Want a better marriage? Speak it! Want a growing business? Invest your creativity into it! Create the unseen and soon you will have what you have never seen before.

Don't feel it! Faith it!

I have fought a good fight, I have finished my course, I have kept the faith: (I Timothy 4:7)

God didn't call us to a fight of feelings but *the good fight* of faith. Stop infecting your faith with feelings! Don't Feel it! Faith it!

Many say: I feel it! If you live in the realm of feelings held captive by your carnal nature not the Spirit of God, you will of the flesh reap a corrupt twisted life. Yes, emotional feelings are real but not relevant to faith. Don't allow your feelings to subdue your faith. If you live by faith you are released from living by feelings. Feelings are not needed to express faith. If you are waiting to feel something before you exercise faith you will feel nothing but the queasiness of fear. You will cower in a shroud of excuses and fearful complaints dissatisfied and spiritually hungry. If you are waiting for something to appear before you express faith, you will not see anything. Faith sees and believes before it sees.

Think on these things

Now Pray: Lord, deliver me from feeling my way through life and allowing feelings to dictate my actions. I surrender my feelings to faith and free my faith to see, believe, conceive and receive.

Decree a Thing

Thou shalt also decree a thing, and it shall be established unto thee: and the light shall shine upon thy ways. (Job 22:28)

To decree a thing is to declare, implement, and set in order laws of living by the commandments of your mouth. What you say is enacted and executable.

Earlier we mentioned that man is a magnifier, magnifying all that he sees and all that enters his being. We have also mentioned that man is a creator like God and may articulate what he wills to be and see. It is also true that man captures with his spirit, like a camera, the things he focuses on. In other words, he may behold things or hold things in his being, captured by his spirit. For example, you may see and know God as you capture Him with your spiritual eyes and ears.

In addition, man's mouth is the mechanism whereby he creates. Therefore, you must open your mouth to release your creative ability. Many would prefer to muse over things rather than *speak those things!* But you must speak to create.

Have you noticed when you are going through troubling things you become speechless? The enemy of your soul wants you to keep your mouth closed or open it in haste, because by your words you may create your world. Therefore, you must resist the natural tendency to be silent when seas are turbulent. Jesus spoke in the face of a storm. He stilled the storm with His words rather than become silent. Learn the lesson: **During a storm is not the time to keep quiet; it is the time to speak what you will and get what you want!**

Think On These Things

What we say becomes law and is implemented in our lives. What you say you sow, and what you sow you will see. Your mouth is the mechanism by which you plant your present and reap your future.

You may pass sentences of life and death with your mouth. An example of this is parents who speak into their children's lives. Some call their children dumb or say they will be a failure like their father or mother. These words stick fast in their being and become laws, either limiting or liberating but always producing in their lives. How powerfully positive can this process be as opposed to the negative process it has been? Parents are positioned to speak life into their children's lives.

Things that are negative negate good will, well being and purpose. Do not negate the best in yourself or others by negative speaking. Use your mouth to pronounce blessings, to create your world, to enact prosperity, peace and provision. Use your mouth to move your mission and mountains of impossibilities.

When you are practicing prayers of faith, intentionally speak in the present and future tenses. For example, "I AM healthy whole and healed". "All that I have and all that I possess IS covered by covenant with God." "My children ARE a blessing to me and we ARE blessed coming in and going out." "All that I set my hands to IS blessed. All my bills ARE paid; all my debts

ARE resolved." "Wealth and riches ARE in my house and more than enough is in my hands."

In the face of giants and storms, pray the prayers of faith. *For by thy words thou shalt be justified, and by thy words thou shalt be condemned. (Matthew 12:37)* Your words matter and produce the substance of faith.

Now Pray: Lord I will open my mouth wide, fill it with your words.

Reflection 37: Ask God to send His words and when they arrive work the word you heard.

Changing Zones: From Faith to Glory

And a woman having an issue of blood twelve years, which had spent all her living upon physicians, neither could be healed of any, Came behind him and touched the border of his garment: and immediately her issue of blood stanched. And Jesus said, "Who touched me?" When all denied, Peter and they that were with him said, Master, the multitude throng thee and press thee, and sayest thou, Who touched me? (Luke 8:43-48)

By faith we participate in the glory of God. By faith, we gain access to all that is God. *In his presence is fullness of Joy. (Psalm 16:11)* Not only do we experience fullness of joy in His presence, but peace, love, and hope. *In glory* we are made whole, healed, delivered, and prospered to prosper. Every space is filled and every need is met in His glory. God's glory *is* who He is. God is His glory. *The whole earth is full of his glory. (Isaiah*

6:3) Is your world full of his glory?

We live in a world of disease, dysfunction, division, desperation, and disturbance. So did the woman with the issue of blood. But notice that she was depleted but decisive. She was diseased but deliberate in her pursuit of Jesus. We might imagine that her heart was thumping with the prospects of her pursuit as she moved toward Jesus *fighting within and fighting without.* She could have stopped at any point but at some point it became too late. At some point, her faith had exceeded her objections. **Your faith must exceed your well reasoned objections.** In this setting with Jesus, the audience became one and she was the audience. Then suddenly Jesus exclaims, "*Who touched me?" (Luke 8:45)* Jesus knew someone had *really* touched Him because virtue had gone out of Him. However, He also knew that someone was now standing where He was standing, on holy ground. The woman with the issue of blood was now standing in the arena of God in another zone where time does not matter and issues fade. In a multitude of people, she was the only one who gained Jesus' attention. She was the only one subject to His honor. And in subjection to Him, she drew upon Jesus' honor until His honor dried up her issue.

Have you gained God's whole attention? Some of you are trying and He will soon incline His ear to hear your petitions. Like the woman with the issue of blood, you must pursue beyond your boundaries and borders to places uncharted and unfamiliar, until you are healed. You must pursue until all your barriers are breached and limits exceeded. You must pursue beyond your NO parking zones, reserved parking and moving violations-defined as the laws of your being. You must break invisible laws to get to Jesus and participate in His glory.

Our holy effort is to climb up into His glory. The ladder Jacob witnessed of angels ascending and descending is a glimpse of the portal we tread upon and ascend by faith. (Genesis 28:12)

Glory: The Manifestation of who God is
Unseen of God

Faith: How we participate in the glory of God.
Unseen of faith

Fight: The trial of faith in temporary circumstances.
Seen and temporal

The model above shows that before we participate in glory we must graduate from a level of faith. Faith is steps we take before ascending into glory. Therefore, we go *from faith to faith and glory to glory* by faith. You cannot graduate to God's glory or in God's glory until you graduate in faith. If you haven't realized it yet, faith wins a place in His glory. The manifestation of healing and deliverance represent revealed glory, manifestations, and demonstration (revealed glory) of the Spirit of God. *And my speech and my preaching was not with enticing words of man's wisdom, but in demonstration of the Spirit and of power… (I Corinthians 2:4)*

God will draw you to places unseen, unknown, and unfamiliar, by His word and by your desire. He will draw you by you're longing for Him. Whatever your issue, you must participate in God's glory by faith to precipitate his revealed glory or manifestation of the blessing you require.

We must take steps of faith with the goal of winning Christ. Steps of faith move us from glory to glory. If that is the case, then we can all walk on a natural plane in a supernatural way.

Consider further that you cannot have faith without God's word. His word is His order restoring you to His original purposes. God gives us His word so we might apply our faith. His word is His original purpose and intent for all things-including you.

Your fear is the only thing that can keep you from exceeding your need. It is the only thing that can keep you from participating in God's glory by faith.

Now Pray: Lord Jesus, by the fight of faith bid me to come into the places of faith that I may participate in your glory. Until I hear you say, "Who touched me? Or take of your shoes, where you are standing is holy ground."

By the way, wherever God is standing is holy ground. That could be in your house, in your marriage; in your business or any place God is welcomed in your life.

Reflection 38: God touches those who touch Him by faith. Is your condition moving you to act in faith exceeding the boundaries and limitations of your present circumstances? You will know you're ready to touch God when you render your feelings, emotions, objections, and the objections of others unnecessary. The goal is God. Your ceiling must become the floor and God you must adore. What is the need you need to exceed? **Seek God and you will exceed extremes excessively.**

Demonstration: Stretch out your hand and by faith touch the hem of His garment. Whatever is in your hand by faith put it into the arena of glory and there you will have a testimony.

In review: Your mouth is the mechanism utilized to create your life. You are a creator who can magnify whatever you see and hear. Therefore, what you meditate on you will magnify. What you magnify becomes the abundance of your heart. What your heart is abundantly full of you will eventually speak. What you speak you create and what is created is manifested as fruit or results in your life. If you become fixated on failure, failure will be magnified in your life and fill your heart. Then whether consciously or not; audibly or not, you will speak it and create it in your life. Conversely, if you speak positive success into your life it will grow in your heart and show in your life. It will grow and it will show. Here are **10 extra points of light** to reflect upon:

Faith finds a way, fear gets in the way.

Faith will not retreat, fear will not engage.

Faith is only radical to those who are rational.

Faith can, fear never will.

Faith focuses on the word of God, fear focuses on the storm.

Faith finishes, Fear won't get started

Faith isn't risky, it's revolutionary!

Faith has feet, but you must take the steps.

Faith creates, fear deliberates.

Faith takes the fight to the fight, fear takes flight.

Chapter Notes

_____

_____

_____

_____

Let us hold fast the profession of our faith without wavering; (for he is faithful that promised ;)
(Hebrews 10:23)

GIVING PAGES

Pressed Down and Poured Out

Chapter 4

Pressed Down and Poured Out

Give and It shall be given unto you; good measure pressed down, and shaken together, and running over, shall men give into your bosom. (Luke 6:38)

The world is always seeking to get; the life of the Christian is giving. Giving is indeed living. Now some will object that too often people will take advantage of you if you are always giving. This is not biblical. *Whatsoever a man sows; he will also reap. (Galatians 6:7)* The devil knows if you cannot give you cannot live. Therefore, he has used the hurts of many to make them averse to being givers. They are unable to give in order to live. Because you are purposed to give, you must be a giver.

When and why did you stop giving? Have you overcome the temptation to live selfishly? *Give and it shall be given unto you.* Some will say, you do not know my pain, you do not know what I have suffered. It is true I do not know. However, Jesus endured every physical, emotional, and spiritual pain, *who was in all points tempted as we are yet without sin. (Hebrews 4:15)* In other words, what Jesus endured did not cause Him to separate himself from God, purpose, or from you. We do not have a high priest who cannot be touched with feelings of our infirmities. If Jesus gave through pain, so can you.

God knows and is willing to heal your brokenness. You ask, "What must I do?" You must like a wounded soldier come to the healer and let Him pour in oil and wine. He cannot heal what you do not expose. He cannot make whole what you don't confess needs healing. We have asked before and ask again, *Will you be made whole?* This will release you from rehearing and rehearsing the hurt, playing the plaintiff, and excusing your condition. Most of all, you can become a giver. The highest calling we have in life is giving. The places of Jesus' wounds were evidence of a transforming experience and it came through God so loving the world that He gave.

Think On These Things

Your giving may not always be appreciated or reciprocated but always rewarded. In other words, your giving always gives back to you in some form.

>*Now Pray: Lord, I thank you no pain can persist in places you have healed. My scars are evidence of your healing power and now I am whole, healed and a giver of life.*

Reflection 39: Giving is not what you do, it's who you

are. The more you give the more you live. However, your focus should be on giving not living.

When you need nothing God will give everything. He who does not give cannot live and what you sow you will eventually grow in your future.

Do you wake each morning looking for and expecting opportunities to give?

The most successful people have positioned themselves to give to others. They are philanthropist, entrepreneurs or small business owners. They are those who have risked their dreams and resources to give to others. If you are a giver you never need to worry about living. It's a principle that works when you work it. What is that you have to give?

Many are waiting for someone to give them something but the truly prosperous soul is anticipating opportunities to give. How can one give it all and lose nothing? God always rewards giving. *He loves a cheerful giver. (2 Corinthians 9:7)*

Two Mites are More

And he called unto him is disciples, and saith unto them, Verily I say unto you, That this woman hath cast more in, than all they which have cast into the treasury. (Mark 12: 41-44)

The widow woman gave only two mites or a fraction of a penny. Yet Jesus was impressed because He says this woman gave more than all the others who gave. How is that? It is so because she gave with her heart not her hand. She gave herself; she gave her all; she gave her best. By giving everything she consummated covenant with God. It is not what she gave but how she gave it. It was the heart of her giving not what she gave.

God honors the heart of giving therefore you can give a dollar like it is a million dollars. God values what's in your heart more than what's in your hand.

Think On These Things

Do you want to be rich? Then you must become poor. You must give your way into great wealth and success. *His ways are not your ways; his thoughts are higher than your thoughts.* (Isaiah 55:8-9) **Do life God's way and give!** Give to Live! Giving *is* living. The more you give; the more you live. *Give and it shall be given unto you.*

Reflection 40: Should you give until it hurts? No, give until the need is met. Jesus gave until He was dead and that met our need to live. On the other hand, to spend your life on yourself is to become poor at last.

We Have This Treasure

Labor not to be rich: cease from thine own wisdom. (Proverbs 23:4)

Many people are worn by the ritual of being busy. Many are marching for money. Many are chasing illusive success. It is a deceptive practice that entices many to create a busy lifestyle in pursuit of success and money.

To gain true riches, motion must be guided by purpose, pursuit by passion and success obtained by maximizing one's inner potential. You will eventually exhaust your most courageous efforts, if you mistake motion for mission, pursuit for progress, or sums of money for success. Start with the premise that you are already rich.

How many are tired of chasing money? Too often, if one captures money he loses value. He is surprised to find it an empty gain. How many are taxed by the prospects of being rich, only to find riches may render one bankrupt? And after all, this pursuit of riches is a pursuit of getting not giving.

You must turn within and find true treasure. *We have this treasure in earthen vessels. (2 Corinthians 4:7)* You must identify and value the gift leaping within you. It has eternal value. Your eternal being will never be satisfied with temporary riches. *There is a way which seemeth right unto a man, but the end thereof are the ways of death. (Proverbs 14:12)*

Are you pursuing you? Or are you pursuing money and success? Success is the pursuit of God's best and doing what you were created to do. It is measured by maximizing your purpose in God. True success is manifesting God's best in you for His name sake and glory.

Many people are busy but not productive. Many are busy but not becoming. They possess money but are not happy. The truth is that you become rich by investing your eternal capital in time. Time is for purpose and should not be exchanged for money forever.

Think On These Things

What is *in you* that cannot be denied? What is *in you* with regards to your purpose that is priceless? What do you possess in your being that cannot be purchased? What is in you that cannot be sold for equal value. To be truly wealthy you must give the eternal possessed within you and give it unconditionally.

The world will try to minimize you, steal your true value and entice you to exchange money for mission. Do not sell purpose for *thirty pieces of silver* when you can live out of your inner treasure and abundance.

The point is: What is in you is more valuable than the things you may be running to. You are being drawn to a higher calling. Your meaningful mission is priceless and precious. It supersedes any earthly accomplishment or dollar amount.

On the other hand, if you would master life and fulfill purpose, you may find it comes without applause. You can't count it, and effort is only one part of it. It is God's doing. *This is the Lord's doing and it is marvelous in our eyes. (Psalm 118:23)* It is His process to reveal in you His purpose that it might be to His glory.

> *Lord, help me to value the truth that I am already rich waiting to be spent and become truly wealthy.*

Reflection 41: Start working on you and success will find you.

Imagine yourself full of success. Imagine millions are within you already. Imagine that the real pursuit of success is within you not outside of you or in others. This is the great excavation of your soul and spirit appointed to you to be manifested in time.

The Tithe: Divine Dimes

Bring ye all the tithes (dimes) into the storehouse, that there may be meat in mine house, and prove me now herewith, saith the Lord of hosts, if I will not open you the windows of heaven, and pour you out a blessing, that there will not be room enough to receive it. (Malachi 3:10)

And

One tenth of the produce of the land, whether grain from the land or fruit from the trees, belongs to the Lord and must be set apart to him as holy. (Leviticus 27:30)

A tithe is a tenth of all your increase. A tithe is a dime of every dollar. When you bring in all the dimes, God receives the tenth and counts it as though you gave it all. This faith action consummates covenant with God and causes you to be blessed. Covenant is more than a contract or agreement it is selling out and giving all. Covenant requires giving all for all. Covenant isn't just giving something but rendering everything. In giving to God we give all we have, for all He has. We give everything *we are* for everything *He is*.

In tithing we bring a dime of all to God and

consummate covenant. The dime belongs to the Lord. Many argue that tithing is an Old Testament practice that is not to be practiced by the New Testament church. Or they offer the argument that this was the practice of an agricultural society. To them we ask: Is giving and worship in the New Testament? Has it changed that we must put God first in everything? Has it changed that we are to honor God above all? What makes the worship of tithing as relevant today as it was throughout the bible is that it still honors God first.

You may ask: what If I don't bring God my dime? Then don't expect the windows of heaven to be opened, for God to pour you out a blessing you have no room to receive or for Him to rebuke the devourer for your sake. In my opinion, that is too much covenant coverage to forfeit.

> *It is a snare to the man who devours that which is holy, and after vows to make inquiry. (Proverbs 20:25)*

Would you expect a return on an investment if you didn't consummate the investment? It is true, you may opt out of tithing but that steals God's honor and robs you of the blessings of covenant with God. Who doesn't want God in their finances, family, and future? The blessing of tithing is that through tithing God invest himself in your life and finances.

> *Honor the lord with your capital and sufficiency [from righteous labors] and with the firstfruits of all your income. (Proverbs 3:9*

Amplified)

God does not need your money; He desires your heart. *For where your treasure is, there will your heart be also. (Matthew 6:21)* Is your treasure with God? Then your heart is with God. God knows if He has your heart then He has your treasure. If He has what is in your heart; He has what is in your hand. When you honor Him first through tithing, what flows out of God, who is eternal, flows overwhelmingly into your life to meet your temporal needs.

Think On These Things

Will a man rob God? If the question is asked then it must be possible that a man will rob God. How is this possible? A man may rob God in tithes and offerings.

Reflection 42: Very simply, can you give God all? God will not force you to bring your dime nor should anyone. But you must know that God wants to *Open to you the windows of heaven and pour you out a blessing.* If this is not appealing then you may default on bringing your dime but don't expect the blessing.

To clarify, we don't pay tithe as it were debt. The dime belongs to God and we bring it as an offering. We are offering to God what is already His. By the way, this is not to be argued over. Either you will bring God an acceptable tithe with a sacred heart or not. The question is: **If you cannot honor God with a tithe, do you really honor God?**

My advice is that you honor God with the first of all you have. Give God what is His and He will give you all He has. Give God your heart through your dime and He will give you the treasures of heaven. Give God what you CAN see and He will give you what you have NEVER seen. What you give God exceeds your capacity to receive. As He gives the increase, *there will not be room enough to receive it (the blessing).*

Abraham gave God a dime of all, and he was rich, very rich, and would not even deny God his only son. *Take now thy son, thine only son Isaac, whom thou lovest, and get thee into the land of Moriah; and offer him there for a burnt offering. (Genesis 22:2)*

Like Abraham, we must give our way into worship. Giving is the first of worship. Worship means to become one with the object of your worship. The object of our worship is God. And like Abraham we worship God with our first, our only and our all.

Think On These Things

Where God is first, He is honored. When He is honored He flows into your heart and life. God's flow in your life will cause you to prosper and overflow into the lives of others. It is an inescapable cycle of blessing!

What shall I render unto the Lord for all his benefits toward me?
(Psalm 116:12)

Reflection 43: What do you owe God? You owe Him

exactly everything but He only requires a tenth which is holy. He takes that dime and applies it in heavenly places and counts it as though you gave the whole dollar. For those who are worried about tithing and not meeting your debt obligations, it is worth restating that:

I have never seen the righteous forsaken or his seed begging bread. (Psalm 37:25)

In other words, giving to God has never caused anyone to go hungry or lose possessions. The opposite is true because when you give to God, He then invest himself in your giving. We will explore the "in" principle later in this writing to establish this truth. Giving to God has never impoverished anyone. Give God an opportunity to bless you and bring in all the dimes! **The tithe is for worship not worry.**

After reading this section, journal all the benefits you have experienced through tithing. It's easy to give ritually without engaging the worship of tithing. List what God has done for you as one who tithes and thank Him for all His benefits. For those of you not tithing, find someone who does and ask them how they have benefited. Or if you're really adventurous, prove God in this area and bring in all the dimes! And if you do, *Blessed shalt thou be in the city, and blessed shall thou be in the field. (Deuteronomy 28:3)*

What's Love Got To Do With Giving?

Therefore as the church is subject unto Christ, so let the wives be to their own husbands in every thing. Husbands, love your wives, even as Christ also loved the church, and gave himself for it. (Ephesians 5:24, 25)

The greatest love of all is giving. The nature of love is to give and giving is the greatest love of all. *For God so loved that he gave.*

Marriage is an area of great challenge in giving. Giving in marriage is a big test for many.

Do you recall that Sarah called Abraham Lord? (I Peter 3:6) Why did she say that? She said this because she honored Abraham and submitted to his authority under God. She did this because she understood that giving is love and love is worship meaning to become one with another. In reality, by submitting to Abraham she was submitting to God.

Today, we could not imagine a woman calling her husband Lord. Why is that? It is so because submission and honor have been perverted in our society to mean "inferior to" or "lesser than". Of course, if it means that, then who wants to submit to or worship their spouse under those terms? It is unfortunate but true.

The scriptures mention *submitting yourselves one to another in the fear of the lord. (Ephesians 5:21)*

The greatest honor a woman may experience is to be submitted to her husband. The greatest honor a man may experience is to be submitted to his wife through love. Love and submission are the same. Love for the man is submission for the woman. It appears God commanded for each partner to do what is most difficult for each.

Watch this: **If the enemy can siphon honor out of relationships he can introduce war and combat in marriage.** We must honor one another in marriage. We must love one another and this will cause marriages to not only survive but thrive. If each party is not honored unconditionally, needs go unmet, relationships suffer and couples begin to make a case for divorce.

There is indeed a measure of worship in love. Love is an exchange between two parties. It requires giving. In worship we give until we're one with the other party. In marriage we give until we're one with our spouses. And because marriage is a covenant relationship, you must give all not least of all. The only way to truly consummate covenant is to give your best; to give your all. Some are objecting at this truth as you read it because you feel you have already given all. Remember, you don't stop giving until the need is met. Is the need of your partner met? Also remember, that you have an eternal unlimited capacity to give because your spirit is eternal. This means in martial relationships, we can give until needs are met not when we have had enough of giving.

God gave us Christ and the church as a model for marriage and giving. Jesus gave his life for the church, which is love. Are you willing to give until you are submitted and one with your spouse?

Let's revisit the subject of submission. All submission means is to position yourself to become one with another party. When the man loves and the woman loves through submission they are one under God. Now clasp your hands together and intertwine your fingers. Your right hand is the man and your left hand is the woman. Now tell me which hand is inferior and which is superior? Would you say your left hand (the woman) submitted to your right hand (the man), is inferior to the right hand? No they are one and neither is superior or inferior. God's will and way is that man and wife would make one new man. He created man as one both male and female created He them.

The devil's number one device is division. He intends to divide and conquer marriage through our thinking. He wants the woman to hear submitted as "inferior to" or the "weaker vessel" as weak. He wants the man to fear disrespect from his wife and force submission, out of fear not love. Unfortunately, this has happened in many relationships and submission no longer holds a weight of honor but rebellious anarchy. Do not allow the devil to rob you of the beauty and blessings of submission and love.

Oh wife, your position of submission is the only place of blessing and prosperity for your life. It releases you into a full life. You will never be more blessed in loving submission to your man. Oh husband, you will never be so blessed in loving submission to your wife under the authority of God.

Wives think of submission as positioning yourself to receive more beauty from your husband. Think of him pouring more and more beauty into you and on you until death do you part. Husbands think of your wife pouring more and more handsomeness into you and on you until death do you part. Think of her pouring out more good looks into your spirit and soul. This is the power of submission and love. This aligns your marriage with God's purpose for marriage which is for two to become one in flesh and spirit.

Now the process of two becoming one is a process not experienced immediately but over time. And it requires three to make a marriage go right. It demands you, your spouse and God to experience success in marriage. The world of marriage apart from God is disadvantaged and often fails because parties do not include God, the author of marriage. Of course, many Christian marriages fail too and that is often the result of being Christians who do not conduct marriage according to God's word.

Sometimes people wonder why a couple who has been married for 35 years would divorce. The answer is because they have had 35 years to make a case for divorce. Over those 35 years enough evidence has been weighted to justify divorce. The two parties have come to a mutual decision based on the evidence collected that the relationship is not worth honoring anymore. The problem with these estimations is that God is able to introduce "God evidence" that the marriage *can* work. Although many can no longer find a reason or cause to stay married, God can flood enough love into your hearts to save your marriage. He can give you, *The love of God shed abroad in our hearts by the Holy Ghost. (Romans 5:5)*

What about unfaithfulness you ask. Many couples even after cases of infidelity have maintained their relationship. How do they do that? It requires a decision to make marriage work as well as forgiveness and healing to restore trust. If you chose to, you can stay married through anything. This writing doesn't address every situation that could sabotage the success of marriage or how to maintain a successful marriage. However, nothing can overcome your mutual stand to save your marriage if that is what you choose.

You must make the decision to love

unconditionally and to see problems as third parties in your marriage. Take the approach that neither one of you is the problem but come together and address the problem as one. When you try to win arguments, you ultimately lose the relationship. Why? If your spouse is made wrong and you are right, the relationship becomes wrong. Similarly, if you are proven wrong, and your spouse is right, the relationship is still wrong. However, if you both attack and address what is wrong, and win, then you're both right and your relationship wins! In other words, avoid winning at the expense of making your partner wrong. This will lead to losing your relationship and the devil wins. All of this requires love, which is giving, when giving is the last action you might want to take.

Think On These Things

Undoubtedly, there are many offenses that plague marriage. They can be forgiven so chose to forgive that your relationship might live. And remember you too have been offensive. It is impossible that you have not- even if unconsciously, done something to offend your spouse. Check the beam in your own eye first. (Luke 6:42)
Remember earlier in this writing we discussed the importance of forgiveness as a means of freeing your heart to be fruitful. As married couples we must live with an attitude of forgiveness and be swift to forgive.

Couples prayer: *Lord help us to love one another as you loved us and die to ourselves that* *we may give ourselves totally to one another in marriage. We understand that as long as we are giving our marriage is living. Lead us to forgiveness no matter the offenses. Lord you love marriage and so do we. We will fight for it unconditionally!*

Reflection 44: Wives, can you like Sarah, worship your husband? These are strong words right? Can you man, die for your wife? Or love your wife as yourself? If so, there is nothing that can sabotage love and marriage.

Husbands your wives need to be released or sanctioned by your weight or authority in God. Wives your husbands need your validation to be what you need them to be. **We cannot fulfill our potential as couples without one another's sanction and validation.** Your role is important to the eternal purpose of your spouse. Give and grant them sanction for success.

The Love of Money

For the love of money is the root of all evil: which while some coveted after, they have erred from the faith, and pierced themselves through with many sorrows. (I Timothy 6:10)

We cannot have a loving exchange with money. Money can't give or receive. Therefore, the love of money is an inappropriate relationship with money. Further, to be subject to money and the chase for money is to allow it to become a god in our lives. Indeed, to love money is to make an idol of it. In reality, money should be subject to us not we to money. Money can't buy you covenant. But God through covenant covers all our needs.

But thou shalt remember the Lord thy God: for it is he that giveth thee power to get wealth, that he may establish his covenant which he sware unto they fathers, as it is this day. (Deuteronomy 8:18) We are empowered to acquire wealth which is wholeness in ever area of our lives. Money is a poor substitute for the riches of glory. We are to master money, not allow ourselves to be mastered by it and know that money is only one measure of wealth.

Many in the church world believe Christians should be poor and have nothing. This is flawed fearful Christianity. How can we operate in covenant relationship with God without the substance to give? How can we fulfill the vision of God's Kingdom and publish the gospel without the resources to do so? And why is being fabulously wealthy an option for those outside the church but not those in the church. Why should we struggle and refuse to be wealthy? This thinking is born out of fear and the belief that "the love of money" will corrupt.

Remember, what you believe you conceive. If you believe you should be poor, you will conceive poverty. If you believe you should live by a certain income you will conceive and receive that income faithfully. This explains why some people get a new job paying more money and still cannot meet their financial obligations. Why? Because they believe for a certain level of living, they conceive it and receive it in spite of their increased income. It's the pauper's phenomenon. No matter how much their income increases, their debts stay the same or increase. Therefore, they still don't have enough to meet their obligations. This explains why people win the lottery and find themselves worst for their winning. **You must have a vision for provision or it will be wasted.**

Do you know that the fear of money will keep money from you? It's not the money that is the matter; it's the heart of the person that needs to be examined. A person with godly intentions may have all the money they need and want. The only stipulation is that they don't make money their god.

Many do believe that pastors want their money when an appeal is made to bring tithes and give offerings. Please dismiss the charlatan paranoia and consider offering time an opportunity to give to God liberally and hilariously. If some church or leader steals what you have purposed for God, they will answer to God. You're not called to hold them accountable. Your position is to present your gift in honor of God.

Think On These Things

Put your money where your heart is. Without fail, you will always put your money where your heart is. Now check your recent purchases or your checkbook and bank statements. You will find your heart there too.

If you love God more than money; you will have all the money you could ever have. God is not opposed to you possessing money; He is opposed to money possessing you. He wants you more than He wants your money! And if He has you, He has your money.

We should have more than enough money and resources. Why? We should be the distributors of wealth and the possessors of it. As distributors of wealth we should have more than enough to overflow into lives of others. It's within your power to have more than enough substance to fill the needs of others. Millionaire status may not be enough for you, but seize it anyway!

Now Pray: Lord, I thank you that I am the master of money and not mastered by it. I thank you that I have the authority to speak to the material by immaterial faith and see what I say materialize. I declare I am debt free and money is serving me, in Jesus name, amen.

Reflection 45: Do you know you may create a flow of money? How is that so you ask? Faith is immaterial; money is material. The entire material world was and is created by the immaterial unseen world. The material world is subject to the immaterial unseen. The things which ARE were created by the things that are not evident. You may call a flow of money into existence to serve your needs. Everything in the material world responds to faith. Do you have faith the size of a mustard seed? Then you can say to whatever mountain it is, be removed.

A mountain is material and can be moved by immaterial faith. Perhaps you could tell the mountain of debt you face to be removed! This works because the unseen immaterial realm is a higher order than the seen material realm. We know this because *the things which are seen were created by things that do not appear. (Hebrews 11:3)*

Become an Offering

And being in Bethany in the house of Simon the leper, as he sat at meat, there came a woman having an alabaster box of ointment of spikenard very precious; and she brake the box, and poured it on his head. (Matthew 26:7; Mark 14:3; Luke 7:37)

What's in your alabaster box? The alabaster box represents the outer casement of your heart. It must be broken. In life we are pushed and pressed so that God might divest us of self and gain our best. God must tilt you to pour you out. Yet, the more you pour the more He restores.

Tilted: To move or shift so as to lean or incline; to tip; also to slant; slope.

When you've reached your limit keep pouring. You must divest yourself of self to invest yourself in God. If you have nothing you can still give God everything. The woman with the alabaster box bestowed upon Jesus her glory. She gave Him the priceless and precious. More than oil was flowing out of her, she was pouring her very self. She was giving God her glory by honoring Jesus.

How can you give God everything when you have nothing? You must pour yourself out and give God the immaterial you. We can only give God the immaterial unseen because He is an unseen God. Even when we give God what we *can* see, like our money, we are really giving Him what is not seen-our hearts. What we cannot measure, the heart, God measures and values most important.

In the account of the woman with the alabaster box, many in that setting focused on what the woman was giving. The real value was in what they could not see her giving. What she gave out of her heart perfumed the room. She poured out the beauty of glory on Jesus making him more glorious in that setting. This required that she humbled herself in His presence. This humility was born out of her condition. And although she was a woman with a bad reputation; she was still endowed with glory.

Learn the lesson: No matter what you've done; you still have the capacity to glorify God. God uses and does not refuse your past, present, and future. He strategically uses each period of your life to make you an offering. He uses trauma and disaster to tilt you and pour you fully for His glory (excellence).

God is attempting to extract the precious ointment in your earthly vessel. He desires your oil for light, which will become an expression of His glory.

You may consider yourself insignificant and unworthy, just pour. You may consider yourself poor, keep pouring. You may have little in your hands; pour what's in your heart. Give yourself and nothing less. *Blessed are the poor in spirit: for theirs is the kingdom of heaven. (Matthew 5:3)*

How can you be poor and afford the kingdom? When you have nothing, give God everything. Give Him yourself in quality and quantity. Give yourself in quotients of glory. Give the treasures of your heart and you will be rich. *Ho, every one that thirsteth, come ye to the waters, and he that hath no money; come ye, buy, and eat; yea, come, buy wine and milk without money without price. (Isaiah 55:1)*

Think On These Things

In this season God is asking you to give Him something to bless. Prepare in your hand a gift that represents the worship in your heart. Like the Widow woman in (II Kings 4:1-38), you can be empty yet full by continually pouring. You can become rich by giving more than you have to pour. Or like the rich young ruler in (Luke 18: 18-23) you can become poor and empty by being full of yourself. **Where there is too much of you very little of God and true prosperity will be found.**

How hard it is for a rich man to enter heaven? It is like a camel passing through the eye of a needle. (Matthew 19:23, 24) What Jesus meant was when the heart is full of self aggrandizement and possessed by riches, it is too full to be filled or receive the kingdom of God.

Jesus was tilted and poured out at the cross. He became an offering poured out for all. *Yet it pleased the Lord to bruise him; he hath put him to grief: when thou shalt make his soul an offering for sin, he shall see his seed, he shall prolong his days, and the pleasure of the Lord shall prosper in his hand. (Isaiah 53:10)*

In many circumstances it appears God has forsaken us. **God cannot leave you; He is eternally invested in you.** He is allowing circumstances to circumcise your heart, so like Mary; you may choose that good part. His process is producing the precious out of your earthen vessel. *Think it not strange the fiery trial that is to try you as though some strange thing has happened. (I Peter 4:12) Many are the afflictions of the righteous* because afflictions tilt you for pouring.

Examine this statement: If I had nothing I would give God everything.

The "In" Principle

Whatsoever God is in becomes like God. God is eternal and abundant in His being. He is overflowing and extreme. Whatever God is in becomes abundant, whole, excessive, overflowing and extremely blessed.

God in a barren womb is a baby; God in the world is the savior. God in you and me is salvation. Whoever or whatsoever God is in becomes like Him.

In the bible we have the account of a man who was blind. (John 9:6) Jesus asked him what he wanted. After he expresses his desire to be healed, Jesus spits on the ground and makes mud. Then He applies the mud to the man's eyes. This man was healed and gained his sight. *He gives sight to the blind. (Luke 4:18)* When Jesus spat on the ground and made mud, the God standing before the man, was now in the mud, and the God in the mud was applied to his eyes. As a result, this man experienced healing.

No matter how undignified the process, we must obey God's word to become one with His word and receive the fruit of His word. God cannot enter your life or circumstances if you are repulsed at the thought of a muddy situation. **If you can get pass the muddy process you will be blessed.**

Naaman in (II Kings 5: 1-19), was instructed to dip in the muddy treacherous Jordan River. He would have preferred a hot tub in a palace but this was God's process not his own. God required of him humility before honor. He demanded his obedience not his sacrifice. After his humiliation, he obeyed and came away healed of leprosy. How did that happen? God was in the muddy Jordan River process not some hot tub in a palace. **Meet God at the point of his word and He will get into your situation.**

What you need more than anything is God involved in every area of life. He will bless the areas you have obeyed Him in. He turned water to wine by the obedience of those present. Likewise, five loaves and two fish became enough to feed a multitude. Why? God responded to those who obeyed His word and got "in" limiting circumstances.

Do you want God in every area of your life? **God gets in where He is obeyed.** God in your finances is an overflow of income. God in your house is a blessed home. God in your ministry is a mission and vision for generations. God in your marriage is a true marriage overflowing with unconditional love, wisdom and understanding.

When you obey God your nets will break with the weight of your increase.

Think On These Things

How do you get God "in"? Wait to see what He will say and then obey.

If you look at things that have removed God or keep God out, you will find disorder, dysfunction, disease, and disaster. For example, when shrewd politicians tried to remove God out of the schools, almost immediately there began to be a rash of school shootings. Similarly, policy makers insist upon separation of church and state. And we all know what the state of the state is. The truth is whatever is void of God lays barren and *without form and void* as the world was in the beginning. Where God is omitted we are left in desperation.

Why ban God when He is more than enough. He is able to do *exceeding above all we can ask or think.* When we omit Him we become subject to temporary elements and die trying by our own efforts. We cannot live successfully where God is omitted.

Now Pray: God I desire you in every area of my life. Give me your word that I might obey you for success.

We often expect God to speak again but He has already spoken and is waiting on our obedience. He will not speak again until you have obeyed the word you have already heard. Have you obeyed God to love your wife as Christ loves the church? Have you obeyed Him to "train up" your children in the way they should go? Have you obeyed God to bring in all the dimes? Have you obeyed Him in all areas of your life?

Have you cast your nets after a long night of toiling?
Have you dipped your pride in muddy Jordan?
Have you poured your heart without measure?
Have you laid up for yourselves, treasure in heaven?

Chapter Notes

_____

_____

_____

_____

And Jesus answered and said, Verily I say unto you, There is a man that hath left house, or brethren, or sisters, or father, or mother, or wife, or children, or lands, for my sake, and the gospel's. But shall receive an hundredfold now in this time, houses, and brethren, and sisters, and mothers, and children, and lands, with

persecutions and in the world to come eternal life. (Mark 10:30)

PURPOSE PAGES

Prove it!

Chapter 5

Prove it!

To everything there is a season, and a time to every purpose under the heaven... (Ecclesiastes 3:1)

And they took him, and cast him into a pit: and the pit was empty, there was no water in it. (Genesis 37: 24)

In this passage of scripture, Joseph was in the pit which meant his purpose was in the pit. This meant Joseph would rise out of the pit because **eternal purposes cannot be bound by temporal circumstances.**

Joseph's situation did not appear to be working for him. He was in a pit when he was really called to a higher purpose. He was bound and left for dead but God still wanted to quicken him to an abundant life.

How many of you are assessing exactly how you arrived in your pitiful situation? How many of you have assessed that your situation must be your destination? How many are reasoning that your pit is your plight?

Can any good come out of what you're in? Yes, there is good in a pit as it relates to God's purpose for your life. *For our light affliction, which is but for a moment, worketh for us a far more exceeding and eternal weight of glory. (2 Corinthians 4:17)*

Believe it or not, the things working against you are light afflictions. Please don't make them heavier than intended. Trouble doesn't last always so don't accept a permanent pit. And remember, whatever you're going through is working for you. **The weight of glory you possess in God is weightier than anything you face in life.** Furthermore, events in life are neither good nor bad they are transitional or transformational as it relates to God's purpose for your life. They are working out what you are about. Whatever your facing today, define it as neither good nor bad but transitional (temporary) and transformational (life changing). **What's in you will graduate you through whatever you are going through. And it will graduate you *to* what God has called you to do.**

And we know that all things work together for good to them that love God, to them who are the called according to his purpose. (Romans 8:28)

Think On These Things

Is it God's fault or God's favor that finds you in a pit? Is it your worst or is it His will? Have you been "abandoned in" or "assigned to" the pit you're in?

It's common that hidden within a problem is a

beautiful answer. If you avoid the problem, you might unwittingly miss the answer. *It is because the thing is established by God, and God will shortly bring it to pass. (Genesis 41:32)*

Now Pray: Lord I thank you that I have been processed through rejection. Rejection has pushed me beyond a pit and a prison to a purpose in a palace. You know the way that I take and are purifying me on purpose. But he knoweth the way that I take: when he hath tried me, I shall come forth as gold. (Job 23:10)

Reflection 46: Children often ask on long trips, when will we get there? Are we there yet? The children of Israel wandered in the wilderness and a generation was lost to impatience and ungratefulness. We must heed this example and wait with patience on destiny to be fulfilled.

Purpose is eternity fulfilled in time. There will be no destiny before it's time. *It is not for you to know the times or seasons, which the Father hath put in his own power. (Acts 1:7)* God has put the fulfillment of your purpose in His own power. Like Abraham, when you become impatient you will likely sow an Ishmael instead of an Isaac. Be careful to wait patiently on the Lord. You will reap in due season if you don't quit. *And let us not be weary in well doing: for in due season we shall reap, if we faint not. (Galatians 6:9)*

Recognize that your timing isn't God's timing. A beautiful song must not only have melody and harmony; it must have rhythm. You're about to reap. Don't choose a rhythm discordant with God's predestined purpose for your life.

Some get married hurriedly. Some start ministry years before its time. **Purpose without timing is like music out of rhythm. It is discordant and hard to endure.** Do not accept an Ishmael; you need Isaac the son of promise. Do not settle for the acceptable will of God when you can enjoy the fullness of His perfect will. You may have labored a long time; don't allow the impatience of elapsed time to push you one inch outside the will of God.

Reflection 47: Know your season and it will alleviate frustration and impatience. Attempting to do the right thing at the wrong time is an avoidable, self-inflicted ailment. *I waited patiently on the Lord; and he inclined unto me, and heard my cry. (Psalm 40:1)* Wait patiently on purpose to be fulfilled in your life.

Buried Talent

And unto one he gave five talents, to another two, and to another one; to every man according to his several ability; and straightway took his journey. (Matthew 25:15)

In this writing, we will use talent to mean anything that has value as it relates to God's invested purpose in each of us.

The unfaithful servant in (Matthew 25) possessed 1 talent and buried his Lord's money. The talent was given to him so he might give, serve, and be a blessing to others. He held value and embodied God's best. Out of fear he admits he buried his Lord's talent and when the lord of that servant returned he had not produced any more value. In so many words, the Lord of this servant said the servant could have at least taken the money to the stock market and made an investment that would have drawn interest. He could have purchased a safe commodity or stock and made more of what was given him. By the way, buried and talent should not go together.

Are you burying your talents in fear? Talents meaning the value of the purpose God invested in you. God has an expectation that whatever He has invested in you He will receive a divine dividend for.

Of course, it was possible that the unfaithful servant in (Matthew 25) could have failed in an endeavor to invest. The market could have crashed, right? But the expectation of his Lord was that he would at least try. The lesson is that you must excuse your excuses and forget reasons you might fail. Deploy your gifts anyway!

How are you going to win if you never play the game? How is your business going to succeed if you never get your product to market and do business? It is God's reasonable expectation that you will at least bring your talents to the marketplace. Why sit until you die? If you die, die trying but please make an effort. **If you're not making mistakes; you're not even trying.**

What are you sitting on? What talent or thing of value have you buried in the backyard of reasonable doubt and fear? No one will benefit from the business you never started. No one will benefit from the book you never wrote. God will not be glorified by the sermons you never preached! If fear is an issue, do it afraid!

Notice in this account of the stewards in (Matthew 25), God doesn't make us responsible for the increase only the effort to present what we have. He doesn't require what we don't have. He requires what He has given us to give. **Use what you have to get where you're going.**

Stewardship is what you do with what you have been given. The Lord of the servants in (Matthew 25) gave to the one who had five talents five more. And to the one who had two talents, two more. But to the one who buried his talent he took that from him and gave it to another who was more faithful and enterprising. God will increase you because of your faithful pursuit of purpose. And when you're faithful God will pursue you with increased stewardship. He gives to those who are giving. He moves those who are in motion. He uses those who are using what they have. He removes those who won't move.

Think On These Things

Now Pray: Lord Jesus, I believe in the treasure you have put in my earthen vessel and choose to make it a blessing for your name sake and your glory.

Reflection 48: God wants the best in you to be exposed to the world so He may be glorified in you. Stop hiding! God knows you and He knows what He deposited within you. What will it cost you to try? Alternatively, what will it cost you to bury your treasure? It will cost you too much. It will cost you great success and blessings.

What of Your Dreams?

All things are possible to them that believe. (Mark 9:23)

Keep dreaming the impossible; the impossible is not really a dream.

A dream is always countered by a dream-killer. There will always be an obstacle to the scared hope seeded in your spirit by God. The majority of people are resistant to what they can't see. Every dreamer desires someone who can see what they see or at least appreciate it. They want to be sanctioned in what they see and believe.

Don't expect the world to dream with you but dream anyway. See more vividly each day what you may become. Hopeless people do hopeless things, keep dreaming. Keep the dream alive before your eyes. Many may look at you critically to dissent and disagree but go on dreaming.

The greatest challenge of dreamers is that those closest to you often have no appreciation for what you're pregnant with. Because they think they know you, they're often too ready to discard the sacred hope you possess. They may dismiss you as they did Jesus, *Is not this Joseph's son? (Luke 4:22)* And because they diminished Jesus on grounds of familiarity, He *could do no great miracles* among them. Understand this, even the most significant people in your life don't see your significance and that's commonplace. The people you may expect to validate you for greatness are often the dissenting voices shouting you down. *Crucify him!* We all want those closest to us to approve us but often this is not the case. Dream anyway!

The Power of Rejection

What God put in you before time from eternity will often be resisted by bandits of unbelievers, unforeseen detours, warring distractions, and ungodly intimidation. People with agendas and reckless entanglements will seek to stop and thwart your divine calling. Fear not, like Joseph, God will use the power of rejection to position you where only God can use you. **It is possible to be exclusive yet excluded.**

It may appear that you are hidden and no one knows who you are. It may seem others are favored and you're not. In truth, you *are* the one favored because you have been set apart by God. Don't get frustrated because you're different. **Different is divine in God.** This means at times you may have to endure what you go through alone. There are times there will be no one near to applaud your efforts or praise your endurance. Eventually God will raise you to prominence like Joseph and sanction you for greatness. God will appreciate what others depreciate and promote you. Promotion comes from God. *For promotion cometh neither from the east, nor from the west, nor from the south. But God is the judge: he putteth down one, and setteth up another. (Psalm 75:6, 7)*

Young Dreamers on the Honor Roll

Like no other population, young people need and require a sacred exchange. They require someone who will bestow their honor upon their honor. They need those who will honor their *being* not only their *doing*.

Our whole society is assassinating dreamers by the millions because we don't understand honor. Our young people are killing themselves in the streets because they're seeking a high grade of honor. **When dreams die; people die.** Many of our young people have lost hope because they're not dreaming. They're not dreaming because their sacred hope (purpose) has been denied. *Hope deferred maketh the heart sick: but when the desire cometh, it is a tree of life. (Proverbs 13:12)*

Endorse the youth in your life. Place honor upon their sacred hope and they will respond like Lazarus coming out of a grave situation. They will be delivered from the streets, drugs, teen pregnancy and a myriad of vices. They will rise on purpose!

Think On These Things

Your dream represents God's sacred purpose in you. When others deny you, God endorses you. When others say no to your dreams and attempt to kill you with their words, God says yes. Understand that man's approval will never promote you neither should you seek men's approval.

Don't allow the dream within you to be amended

or rescinded by others. To stop the dream within you is to stop you or God's sacred purpose for your life. Don't relinquish or allow the dream to be stolen out of your spirit.

Know this, if you keep dreaming, nothing or no one can steal the sacred hope out of your spirit. You will manifest and deliver it! Yes you will! And you will, no matter the situation, always rise on purpose. The dream within you will always deliver you, promote you and advance you to the place God has called you to. *A man's gift will make room for him and give him a place before kings. (Proverbs 18:16)*

> *Confession: No weapon that is formed against **me** shall prosper; and every tongue that shall rise against **me** in judgment thou shalt condemn. (Isaiah 54:17)*

Reflection 49: Some of you are on the precipice of great things. Your purpose has been frustrated long enough. God has heard your deep groaning of frustration and is prepared to promote you. **Where you're going is predestined, where you're at is preparation.** You're only days away, so don't give up. The best is yet to come. Your wilderness was just as purposeful as your promised land. Begin now to give God thanks for where you are and you will begin to feel hope spring up for where you're going. You will never see this wilderness or your familiar enemies again. It's time! You have graduated because you have a dream!

In honor of Dr. Martin Luther King: A King's Dream

Walls fall rise freedom
Voicing empowerment and civil liberty
We are not free 'til all are free
Blood for color diverse as God
Who created all
Black, white, girl, boy

Onward lives King's dream
Vivid rainbows of humanity
Chiseled Mountains of love
Crafted pilgrims pride we see

Through long dark nights we travel
Slave no more bound under
Beating the drum major's drum
Cutting injustice asunder

From slavery freedom rings
From the Negro, from the shame
From the White house it sings
From the heart of a nation unfeigned
Through cavern through plain by underground train
Every hamlet and hill still needs, King's dream.

Original poem by Rogers J. Greene Jr.

Exposed for Excellence

Paul says I rather glory in my infirmities. (2 Corinthians 12:9)

God has made an eternal deposit of purpose in each of us to be fulfilled in time. God wants to expose you. What does that have to do with purpose? There is treasure in you. There are divine diamonds, godly gold and priceless pearls of purpose and destiny hidden within you. The question is: How do you get it out?

There's a process for you and one for each person so endowed. There's always a process related to purpose. The problem is we are often discomforted by the process because it is God's not our own. God extracts the best of you by exposing you through situations and circumstances of life. He uses a refining process. *The refining pot for silver, and the furnace for gold: but the Lord trieth the hearts. (Proverbs 17:3)* He uses fiery furnaces of life to burnish you and prepare you for display in the world. He intends to produce you a vessel of honor for His glory and that explains why He hasn't left the processing to you. You would not choose the process necessary to perfect you rather what is comfortable and convenient. You would choose what would save your life; He wants you dead first then living.

God will allow you like Jesus to be stretched out on a cross of suffering. He will allow the trouble of this world to process you. You will be exposed. Jesus' most open and vulnerable day of exposure worked God's perfect, acceptable will. He died on purpose. *Therefore doth my Father love me, because I lay down my life, that I might take it again. No man taketh it from me, but I lay it down of myself. I have power to lay it down, and I have power to take it again. This commandment I received of my Father. (John 10: 18)*

Have you received your commandment of purpose? Are you fully engaged in your divine endowment? Are you ready to give what God gave you to give? It has been commanded of you before you were born to deliver on purpose.

Think On These Things

Within you is an eternal supply for a timed life. It is the treasure of purpose. Essentially, this is God's plan for your life. God wants to prove this and present you to the world. God wants to show you off. You must first humble yourself and become submitted to His process. He will raise you up and show you off!

Now Pray: Lord expose me and grant grace to endure the process, prepared for the master's use-his workmanship unto good works! Be glorified in me!

Reflection 50: What's in you is bigger than you. The purpose invested in you must become you. You are God's word on assignment from eternity. He watches over His word to perform it and so He watches over you. His word is His order therefore no one can stop your fulfillment because no one can stop God's word. Before you knew *you* God knew you and ordained you a success. Your success is guaranteed in God.

Say Not I am a Child

Then said I, Ah, Lord God! Behold, I cannot speak: for I am a child. (Jeremiah 1:6)

Your destiny is tied to your identity. You must see yourself as God sees you to be what God has called you to be. Many people don't know who they *really* are because they see themselves through the eyes of their dark past. They forgo the true revelation of themselves for the familiarity of their broken images.

The only way to overcome the mundane and temporal vexations of your God-given purpose is to get a revelation of who you are. However, you must not estimate yourself as you have in the past rather by the way God sees you. This must be done in humility, but it must be done. You will never rise above a right estimation of who you are in God. A lesser view of yourself will keep you grounded-a turkey, not an eagle. We rise on revelation. We ascend on purpose by placing proper value on who we are in God. **You must see yourself as God sees you; to be as God has created you to be.** Without the revelation of who you are, you can never become who God intended.

Do you know that you are finished and now on a journey of fulfilling? The premise that we're being completed is faulty. The premise of purpose is that we are complete while finishing what God has already finished.

Declaring the end from the beginning, and from

ancient times the things that are not yet done, saying my counsel shall stand, and I will do my pleasure. (Isaiah 46:10) God finishes then He starts what He finished. He finished your purpose then started what was finished in you. You're done while doing what God has already finished. *Yea, I have spoken it, I will also bring it to pass; I have purposed it, I will also do it. (Isaiah 46:11)*

Too many are caught on "just". "I'm just a housewife"," I'm just a broker", "I'm just a bread winner" and so on. You're "more than" not "less than" what God created you to be. And you're not *just* any one you're the one God elected.

Do you know that God speaks to us but He doesn't speak to us? That is to say, He *really* speaks to what is in us, calling out of us what He desires to be manifested in the earth. He sees us as we *really* are so He can call us on purpose. For example, while Gideon was hiding God was calling him as He saw him, a man of might and valor.

Jesus asked His disciples, *"Who do men say that I the Son of man am?" (Matthew 16:13)* Jesus did not ask this because He didn't know who He was. He asked this because the disciples needed to know who He was. He later asked, *"But whom say ye that I am?"* and the disciples had different answers. *And Simon Peter answered and said, "Thou are the Christ, the Son of the living God." (Matthew 16:13-17)* and Jesus called him blessed. Simon was blessed because he would eventually rise on the revelation of who Jesus *really* was.

Who do you say Jesus is? Who do you say you *really* are?

Think On These Things

We are all called to our various roles. Men are called to be husbands, and fathers, sometimes ministers. By the way, there is grace for each place. You can't fulfill or fill these roles without God. Women are called to be wives, mothers and sisters, and sometimes ministers and leaders of corporations. What is it that you are called to be and do? What has God commissioned you for? Whatever it is, it must be undertaken with grace. It must be pursued with purpose. You must depend on the one who called you to this work. As you depend upon Him, you will find a rest in your work and a peace in your pursuit, enough to feel accomplished and refreshed in your efforts. Yes, what is in you is bigger than you. But it is you! It is His excellence in power waiting to be revealed. He cannot and will not leave His glory unrevealed in your life. God is committed to your success, are you? Therefore, stop telling God what you can't do. He has already seen you do before time was.

His call places a demand on your eternity. He calls from eternity into time to fulfill purpose. He speaks out of heaven- an eternal place to your spirit an eternal creation. He calls to your secret place, to establish His eternal purpose through you. You aren't merely a man; you're a god-man created in His image and likeness.

For we are his workmanship, created Christ Jesus unto good works, which God hath before ordained that we should walk in them. (Ephesians 2:20)

Now Pray: Lord, help me fully engage my purpose. May I not run from the task as Jonah did. May I not make excuses as Moses, Gideon, and Jeremiah did. Lord, help me to see myself as you see me that I may be what you called me to be-eternally.

Reflection 51: Your sense of insignificance is contradictory to your brilliance. You are no less than God in another form. It may seem too grandiose to believe but it is true. The truth is that He has called you. And because He has called you, you must answer. He has purposed you; you must pursue. He has a plan, abide in His process.

Encounters of the God kind: Significant Others

And it came to pass, that, when Elisabeth heard the salutation of Mary, the babe leaped in her womb; and Elisabeth was filled with the Holy Ghost. And she spake out with a loud voice, and said, Blessed art thou among women, and blessed is the fruit of thy womb. (Luke 1:41, 42)

Mary's salutation caused Elisabeth's baby to leap and Elisabeth's sanction of Mary sanctioned her abiding purpose.

We all need Elisabeths and Marys in our lives especially in difficult times. Mary was a teenager with a ridiculous story of how she became pregnant. She needed someone who knew her from the inside out not the outside only. She needed someone that when they encountered one another, there was witness and sanction. She needed someone who could testify of the good in her when no one could see any good about her. In scandal and ruined reputation; she needed someone whose own purpose leaped at the encounter of another pregnant with purpose.

You need people who cause your baby of purpose to leap. You need people who endorse you with their presence, who validate your existence and your purpose. You need those to whom God has revealed you. You need those who see you as God sees you.

Some of you are aching and pinning to meet your own Elizabeth. You are looking feverishly for those who know you and yet love you. Those whom you encounter and they always build you up. They edify you. They lift you and "get you" when no one else does. They know that holy thing you have from God and are there to help you deliver. Who are those people in your life? Who makes the babe of purpose leap in your womb of faith? Who is with you in the discomfort of carrying purpose? Who is there to help you push purpose out of the birth canal of destiny? Who makes your pregnancy with purpose a joy?

Think On These Things

Now Pray: Lord, give me a Mary and Elisabeth to summons my innermost purpose. Give me someone who knows me intimately and does not judge me. Give me someone who causes me to push out destiny and pace my delivery. Lord, give me a confidant, a keeper, a friend, one of like spirit, In Jesus name, amen.

Reflection 52: You may not find many Marys or Elizabeths in life and ministry. However, we all need someone who speaks to our significance, who draws out our divine calling, and holds us accountable to the call on our lives. Leaders, you must have a God encounter with a significant other in order to successfully deliver your commissioned purpose.

Entrepreneurial: To Create and Generate

He that hath a bountiful eye shall be blessed; for he giveth of his bread to the poor. (Proverbs 22:9)

Man was created to create, worship and love. An entrepreneurial spirit is the spirit of creating. As a creator you must be in the habit of making something out of nothing. In addition, you increase the value of times, things, products, and people. The true entrepreneur has the ability to add value to whatever he puts his hands to. If we all possess the spirit of creating and this is the spirit of entrepreneurial ship, then everyone may create and generate something in their lives beyond a job. **There is a big difference between doing what you were born to do (purpose) and doing what you are bound to do (make a living). To be**

successful in the school of life, one must minor in vocations and major in callings.

You must extract something significant out of your heart, put it in your hands, and add value to it. Each of us can add value to and create something. The problem is that most people aren't in the mode of generating and creating, rather maintaining and duplicating. This suffocates the entrepreneurial spirit and that's why a minority of people are ever considered innovators and revolutionaries.

God is entrepreneurial in that He took a seed, His son and sowed Him to reap the savior and we are saved. He utilized seedtime and harvest to strategically place Jesus in the world as savior of the world. Likewise, get some seed in your hand and allow God to bless it.

The true entrepreneur sets out to accomplish his sacred purpose. He creates and generates business and ministry all revolving around his purpose. Therefore, his pursuit is based on *who he is* not necessarily what he does. The mistake of many is to pursue outside of their purpose. Understand that purpose is always rewarded with provision that promotes success.

It's time for you to make purpose happen in your life. It's time to pursue *you* until *you* are overtaken with purpose. To do this your paradigm must shift from money consciousness to a "create and generate" focus.

One sign that you are wealthy is that ideas and people are working for you. For example, this book should be working while I'm sleeping. You should have something working on your behalf so you can indulge your efforts toward purpose. One hindrance to this process is that many entrepreneurs are isolated, not networked, or uncomfortable soliciting others for aid in their purpose. They are lone rangers. God will give you the desire of your heart but you must include others in that desire. You shine brightest when you're "plugged into" other people. *Be kindly affectioned one to another with brotherly love; in honor preferring one another; (Romans 12:10)*

Think On These Things

Some of you are pregnant with an entrepreneurial idea. Some of you are doubly pregnant carrying twin innovations. You must take your ideas from thought to action. Your thoughts and plans are waiting to be employed on your behalf. Its time to push! Allow God to perfect what is in you. Pursue *you* faithfully.

Now Pray: Lord grant me an anointed push from my innermost being. Develop within me the entrepreneurial spirit to create and generate what you purposed from eternity for me to deliver.

Reflection 53: There is a difference between making it happen and waiting for it to happen. The entrepreneur knows he must make purpose happen. He knows he must create and generate what he wants to see. What can you generate and create? What is at the center of your being waiting for your genius to craft it? What value could you add to the places you already work? Build something with the material of purpose lying within you. Use the tools of creativity to generate and create what you desire.

Are you bored, frustrated or unfulfilled in your work? Remember, **you were created to do the impossible not the mundane.**

Go To the Ant

Go to the ant, thou sluggard; consider her ways, and be wise: Which having no guide, overseer, or ruler, provideth her meat in summer, and gathereth her food in the harvest. (Proverbs 6:6-8)

The entrepreneur, like the ant, gathers business accounts, piles pages until he has a book, delivers newspapers until he has an enterprise, sells ice cream until every national store chain sells his product. He develops relationships until he has a network. He gathers whatever he needs to build his dreams and fulfill his purpose.

Think On These Things

One of the keys to successful entrepreneurial ship in the kingdom of God is to give God something to bless. Most people focus on what they don't have; focus on what you do have and what God has given you. He will increase what you give Him faithfully. The widow woman in Kings said, *I have not a cake, but a handful of meal in a barrel, and a little oil in a cruse. (I Kings 17:13)* She basically said she had nothing and what she had was not significant. The truth is, she *did* have something but did not place much value on it. She counted what she had as insignificant.

God makes the insignificant significant. He adds value to the value less and promotes the lowly. Too often we focus on what we don't have. God isn't concerned with what you don't have. He knows what you *do* have and that what you have is more than enough to give and live. He makes your little much and maximizes the minimum. You too can add your value to purpose and make something worthy. You can add your significance to what appears insignificant and prosper significantly.

Now Pray: Lord, I thank you for the entrepreneurial spirit to create and generate whatever I desire. I thank you for the ideas, people, anointing, and plans, you have sowed in my spirit. May I now sow these in the earth and reap a harvest that leads the world.

Reflection 54: What idea are you holding in your heart which needs to be transferred to your hands for deployment? What is your deepest fear keeping you from your most noble pursuit? Who might you seek to be a mentor or model in this area?

Live Bigger: Pivot on Purpose

Every life can be changed by pivoting on purpose. A pivot denotes a point of change. It means to turn. When an individual lives on purpose they are less likely to turn toward lesser pursuits in life.

You won't have time or the desire to join a gang when you're engaged in your purpose. You will escape the temptations of this world when you know they don't fit in God's plan for your life. You can change and turn your life around when you know what you're living for.

If we can help people discover that eternal thing for which they are called maybe they won't die for lesser desires. Purpose is the thing we are called to live by and die for. A young woman has no reason not to get pregnant out of wedlock unless her purpose is bigger. A young man will inevitably fall into mischief if his purpose doesn't answer for him. We all need something bigger to live for. **If you're not living bigger (on purpose) you will die for anything.** Your purposed passion will provoke you to pursue life and not death.

Have you identified your God-given purpose? The sooner you do, the more fulfilled your life will be. What's in you was prepared and predetermined by God and reflects His will. God had a plan for your life before you were born. The problem is that the devil also has a plan for your life and it is twisted. You must avoid the devil's plan by identifying God's will for your life.

Think On These Things

You have been purposed, now prove it! You are called to prove or present your eternal purpose perfected. Time has been allowed for you to live big and prove what God intended by your life. It's not too late. Many of you think you're too old to live big. Some of you think prison is a sure end to your big life. Some of you think having that baby young is a definite end to your bigger purpose. No! No! No! Use your purpose to pivot or turn towards God's highest call for your life. Who told you it was too late, the devil? Time is subject to eternity, you have time. Live big and pivot on purpose!

Plug into God. You must plug into Him and He will plug into you. Your primary purpose is your pivot point. It is the fulcrum of your future.

> *Now Pray: I will praise thee: for I am fearfully and wonderfully made: marvelous are thy works: and that my soul knows right well. (Psalm 139:14)*

Reflection 55: **To parents:** If your children are becoming what you are; are you pleased with what they're becoming? Are you speaking to them or are you speaking to their purpose? Be careful, calling them out of their purpose is as bad as calling them out of their name.

In pursuing God's purpose you will often need to reposition yourself. God will speak to you as He did to Abraham. Sometimes the places you're comfortable with are too small for the big life God has designed for you. *Now the Lord had said unto Abraham, Get thee out of they country, and from thy kindred, and from thy father's house, unto a land that I will show thee. (Genesis 12:1)*

Notice everything was catered to Abraham. It was his country, his kinfolk, and his father's house. God wanted him to leave the familiar for what required faith. **You must walk by faith to arrive at your promise. You must leave many comfortable places to participate in**

destiny.

    Greatness is not only a matter of God given purpose but a matter of position and repositioning. You can be in the wrong place with the right thing (purpose) and fail to be great. However, if you're in the right place with the right purpose, at the right time, you will be great and very prosperous. You may have already analyzed your purpose, now check your position. In the end, dedicate your life to that which is drastically divine- your purpose!

Live on purpose
Or die for nothing
To be filled
Fill others

Chapter Notes

_____

_____

_____

_____

He hath made everything beautiful in his time: also he hath set the world in their heart, so no man can find out the work that God maketh from the beginning to the end.
(Ecclesiastes 3:9-11)

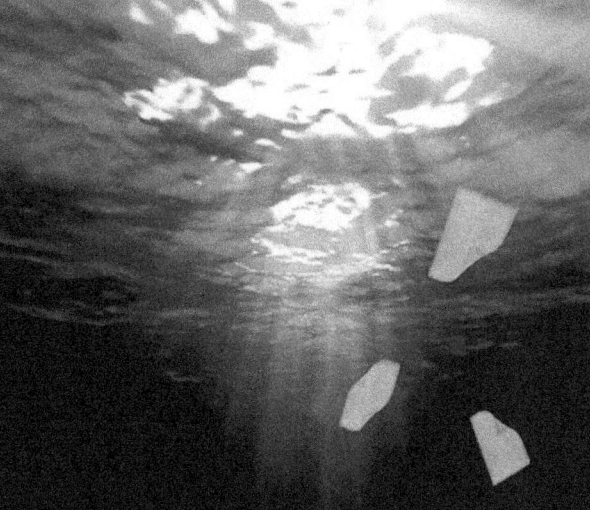

PAGES OF LIGHT

FOR THE PAGES OF YOUR LIFE: VOLUME I

OUR LIGHT IS AN EXPRESSION OF HIS GLORY

WARNING: THIS MATERIAL IS SPIRITUALLY DISCERNED

ROGERS J. GREENE JR.

About the Author

Rogers J. Greene Jr. is a 41 year old native of Louisiana who has lived in the Seattle area for the past 16 years. Rogers is an ordained elder, anointed minister and dynamic speaker who has established himself in the Greater Seattle community as a trusted leader, school teacher, powerful preacher and community advocate. In addition, he holds a B.A. degree in Applied Psychology and certification in Child and Adolescent services from City University of Seattle, a pastoral certification from Dominion College and certification as a School Psychologist with ACSI (Association of Christian School International).

While studying Journalism at Louisiana State University of Eunice, LA he wrote for the school newspaper. He has spoken locally at some renowned area churches and appeared on local radio with KZIZ/KRIZ am of Seattle. In recent years, his advocacy efforts have extended to facilitating Faith-based financial literacy education both locally and nationally, for low income, underserved clients through the Urban League and Casey Family Programs of Seattle.

In his own words:

"My thoughts, writings, and preaching are for those who would resist the inertia of complacency to pursue their destiny with tenacious audacity and godly fervor. My time is for those who refuse to lose until winning is the only option. My advocacy is for those who will defy the gravity of life and ascend to uncommon heights of achievement, prosperity and greatness. My prayers are for those who would give birth to the treasure within them and become eternally wealthy. But more importantly, I aspire to be an example of the believer in word and deed while leading with integrity."

Last Light

It is my prayer that you have been energized, set on fire, inspired, and motivated to pursue your mission. I pray the light of this writing has healed your heart, secured your salvation, fired your faith, embolden your giving and prepared you to manifest your eternal purpose.

God awaits your humble pursuit of him and all things God. Absorb the confluence of light supplied in **Pages of light** to illuminate your church, your family, your community and world for Jesus! Again, thank you for allowing this first volume of **Pages of Light** to fill the pages of your life. And to God be the glory!

The Lord bless thee, and keep thee: The Lord make his face shine upon thee, and be gracious unto thee: The Lord lift up his countenance upon thee, and give thee peace. (Numbers 6:24-26)

COMING IN THE SPRING OF 2012:

Pages of Light for the Pages of Your Life: Volume 2, featuring topics such as: **Effectual Fervent Prayer** and **Angels and Demons.**

For bookings use the following contact information:

Rogers J. Greene Jr.
Email:rjgreene@harbornet.com
Phone: 206-423-4654
Facebook: facebook.com/rogerg2
Twitter: @ rogersjg2

I look forward to meeting you face to face before Jesus comes.

Love

Rogers

www.ingramcontent.com/pod-product-compliance
Lightning Source LLC
Chambersburg PA
CBHW032043150426
43194CB00006B/402